UNIVERSITY CASEBOOK SERIE

2022 SUPPLEMENT TO
BUSINESS ORGANIZATIONS

CASES AND MATERIALS

UNABRIDGED AND CONCISE TWELFTH EDITIONS

JAMES D. COX
Brainerd Currie Professor of Law
Duke University Law School

MELVIN ARON EISENBERG
Jesse H. Choper Professor of Law, Emeritus
University of California at Berkeley

CHARLES K. WHITEHEAD
Myron C. Taylor Alumni Professor of Business Law
Cornell Law School

FOUNDATION
PRESS

© 2020, 2021 LEG, Inc. d/b/a West Academic
© 2022 LEG, Inc. d/b/a West Academic
    444 Cedar Street, Suite 700
    St. Paul, MN 55101
    1-877-888-1330

Printed in the United States of America

ISBN: 978-1-63659-952-6

ANALYTICAL TABLE OF CONTENTS

TABLE OF CASES

The principal cases are in bold type.

UNIVERSITY CASEBOOK SERIES®

2022 SUPPLEMENT TO

BUSINESS ORGANIZATIONS

CASES AND MATERIALS

**UNABRIDGED AND CONCISE
TWELFTH EDITIONS**

CHAPTER 1

AGENCY; THE SOLE PROPRIETORSHIP

2. AGENCY

A. THE AUTHORITY OF AN AGENT

Page 3.* Insert the following before *Esso Geometric v. Harvard Industries*:

Alfaro-Huitron v. Cervantes Agribusiness

United States Court of Appeals for the Tenth Circuit, 2020.
982 F.3d 1242.

HARTZ, CIRCUIT JUDGE. Plaintiffs-Appellants are United States citizens or lawful permanent residents who work as farm laborers. Defendants-Appellees Cervantes Agribusiness and Cervantes Enterprises, Inc. (collectively, Cervantes) are agricultural businesses owned and managed by members of the Cervantes family in southern New Mexico. Plaintiffs brought claims against Cervantes for breach of contract . . . based on Cervantes's failure to employ them after a labor contractor, allegedly acting on Cervantes's behalf, recruited them under the H-2A work-visa program of the United States Department of Labor (DOL). The district court granted summary judgment in favor of Cervantes. . . . [W]e reverse the district court's ruling . . . because the evidence taken in the light most favorable to Plaintiffs is sufficient to support a finding that the contractor was acting as Cervantes's agent when it recruited them. . . .

I. Background

A. Dealings Between the Parties

In September 2011 Dino Cervantes, managing vice president of Cervantes Enterprises and general manager of Cervantes Agribusiness, signed a one-page "Agreement of Outsourcing Support" with labor contractor WKI Outsourcing Solutions, LLC (WKI). The Agreement stated that it was "for services as a work force provider. The work force consists of skilled farm labor workers; U.S. Citizens, legal residents, or foreign workers with temporary working visas (H-2A)." The Agreement was to be "effective from [November 10, 2011] and ending [March 9, 2012], for the following crops: Processing & Packing: Dry Red Chile & Other Spices"; and WKI agreed to "provide 15 farm workers on a daily basis for the length of this agreement." Also in September, WKI entered

---

* In the Concise Edition insert case before *Speed v. Muhanna* at page 3.

1

into materially identical agreements with representatives of three other farm operators and packing companies in southern New Mexico.

The president of WKI, Jaime Campos, had promoted his company to Cervantes and other agricultural businesses as a legal source of foreign labor through the H-2A work-visa program. He believed that farmers were suffering from a lack of reliable labor in the United States and that the H-2A visa program could solve that problem by bringing workers into the country from Mexico. One of the farmers who entered into an agreement with WKI, Ronnie Franzoy, testified at his deposition that he wanted all his labor to come from Mexico partly because he thought Mexican laborers were the most dependable. Mr. Cervantes was also interested in obtaining foreign workers: He testified at his deposition that there would be no reason for him to use WKI's services if WKI were not bringing in foreign workers.

The H-2A visa program established by the Immigration and Nationality Act of 1952, as amended by the Immigration Reform and Control Act of 1986, allows domestic employers to hire nonimmigrant foreign workers for agricultural labor on a temporary or seasonal basis. . . . To obtain permission to hire workers under the program, an employer must establish that it faces a shortage of qualified United States workers and that the employment of foreign labor will not adversely affect the wages and working conditions of similarly employed United States agricultural workers. . . . The program is administered by the DOL, which has promulgated regulations for that purpose. . . . Because the DOL has a "statutory duty to protect American workers," its regulations require employers to "first offer the job to workers in the United States." *Id.* (citing 20 C.F.R. § 655.121). . . . The DOL requires employers to offer at least the highest of the federal or state minimum wage, the prevailing hourly or piece rate, or the adverse-effect wage rate (AEWR) that the DOL sets on a state-by-state basis. . . .

WKI applied for H-2A certification from the DOL in September 2011. As part of this process Mr. Campos submitted under penalty of perjury an Application for Temporary Employment Certification, *see* 20 C.F.R. § 655.130, which stated, among other things, that to the best of his knowledge: (a) "[a]t this time, there are not sufficient workers who are able, willing, or available at the time and place needed to perform the farm labor and services required by . . . farmers [of certain seasonal crops]," . . . (b) workers would be paid the AEWR wage of $9.71 per hour (more than both New Mexico's minimum hourly wage ($7.50) and the federal minimum hourly wage ($7.25) at the time); and (c) qualified United States workers would have priority in hiring, in compliance with federal regulations on the subject, ...

Because WKI was required to make employment available to United States workers first, it began working with the relevant state workforce agencies, including the Texas Workforce Commission (TWC), to recruit

United States workers for the available positions described in the clearance order. . . .

During the recruitment period numerous United States workers expressed interest in WKI's job listings; a person who had worked for TWC for some 40 years testified that she could not remember ever seeing another H-2A application that resulted in so many referrals of qualified United States workers. WKI hired Plaintiffs, all of whom were "United States workers" under the H-2A regulations. . . . Because WKI did not draw up separate written work contracts for each Plaintiff, "the required terms of the [clearance] order and the certified Application for Temporary Employment Certification" became their work contracts. . . .

At some point in November 2011, however, Mr. Campos called Cervantes and "talked to somebody on the farm," leaving a message for Dino Cervantes that the other farms were terminating their work agreements and that WKI "wouldn't do anything against him" if he likewise "had to terminate" the Agreement. . . . In the same vein, on November 22 WKI sent an "EMERGENCY REQUEST" to the DOL seeking to postpone the start date by four months, changing the period of employment for which WKI had been approved to employ farmworkers to March 1 through June 30, 2012. In its letter to the DOL, WKI stated that "the agricultural producers that WKI has contracted with . . . have informed WKI that due to severe drought conditions . . . , there is no work to be performed at this time." . . . On December 1 the DOL granted WKI's request to cancel its H-2A application because of contract impossibility.

According to Mr. Franzoy, who had also entered into an agreement with WKI, its assertion to the DOL that the contracts were canceled due to weather conditions was "a bunch of kahooey." . . . "The reason that [Mr. Campos canceled the H-2A application was] because he wasn't able to get the people from Mexico in our agreement." . . . Mr. Franzoy still "had chile to pick that year," and he "could have used the help and the labor." . . . Presumably, Mr. Campos believed that the farmers with whom he had contracted would not be happy about paying AEWR wage rates for domestic workers.

For the Agreement's effective dates of November 2011 through March 2012, Cervantes met its seasonal labor needs through its longtime labor contractor, Jesus Maldonado, whose workers were paid the state minimum wage for picking chile and other tasks. Neither Cervantes nor WKI provided work to Plaintiffs during the time period for which Plaintiffs were hired under the terms of the H-2A contract.

B. Court Proceedings

Plaintiffs filed suit. . . against Mr. Campos, WKI, Cervantes, and other agricultural employers with whom WKI had contracted. . . . Plaintiffs alleged . . . breach of their employment contracts, [and] violations of the AWPA. . . .

Cervantes moved for summary judgment on all claims. . . . [T]he district court granted the motion on Plaintiffs' claims for breach . . .

On appeal Plaintiffs argue that the district court erred in granting summary judgment in favor of Defendants on their claims for breach of contract. . . .

II. Analysis . . .

A. Breach of contract

Plaintiffs allege that Cervantes breached Plaintiffs' employment contracts . . . because it "fail[ed] to provide any of the promised work" to Plaintiffs during the November 2011 to March 2012 season. . . . Although it was Mr. Campos, not Cervantes, who . . . had direct contact with Plaintiffs, Plaintiffs argue that Cervantes is nonetheless liable because it authorized WKI to act as its agent in recruiting Plaintiffs and therefore can be held responsible by them for any contractual breach. In response, Cervantes contends that the district court correctly concluded that it lacked sufficient control over WKI to create an agency relationship.

We hold that the district court erred in granting Cervantes summary judgment on this ground. As will be explained in more depth below, the "control" test applied by the district court is the test used to distinguish employees from independent contractors, who may or may not be agents. The distinction is important in tort law because employers may be liable for the conduct of tortfeasors who are their employees when they would not be liable if the tortfeasors were not employees but mere independent contractors. But this is a contract claim, not a tort claim. Cervantes may be liable under a contract entered into by Mr. Campos as its agent even though Mr. Campos was not an employee of Cervantes. And although the agency relationship requires some measure of control by the principal, the requisite control is much less intrusive than the control necessary for an employer-employee relationship. In our view, the evidence presented to the district court could support a determination that Mr. Campos was acting as the agent of Cervantes in entering into contracts with Plaintiffs. Therefore, the summary judgment on the contract claim cannot stand. . . .

1. Background agency principles

To resolve this appeal, we need not examine all the intricacies of agency law. We will briefly review some of the fundamental concepts and principles. Then we can focus on the meaning and implications of the principal's authority to control the agent.

We begin with the definition: "Agency is the fiduciary relationship that arises when one person (a 'principal') manifests assent to another person (an 'agent') that the agent shall act on the principal's behalf and subject to the principal's control, and the agent manifests assent or otherwise consents so to act." Restatement (Third) of Agency § 1.01; *see Hansler v. Bass*, 106 N.M. 382, 743 P.2d 1031, 1036 (Ct. App. 1987) ("An agent is one authorized by another to act on his behalf and under his control."); Restatement (Second) of Agency § 1(1) ("Agency is the fiduciary relation which results from the manifestation of consent by one person to another that the other shall act on his behalf and subject to his control, and consent by the other so to act.").

An agent is not simply someone who acts to benefit another person. Anyone who provides services or goods is expected to benefit us. Central to the notion of agency is that the agent acts "on behalf of" the principal. The agent is acting in the principal's stead, as the principal's representative. As stated by the Reporter for the Restatement (Third) of Agency, "[A]gency doctrine defines the legal consequences of choosing to act through another person in lieu of oneself." Deborah A. DeMott, *A Revised Prospectus for a Third Restatement of Agency*, 31 U.C. Davis L. Rev 1035, 1039 (1998). "It has been said that a relationship of agency always contemplates three parties—the principal, the agent, and the third party with whom the agent is to deal." Restatement (Third) of Agency § 1.01 cmt. c (internal quotation marks omitted).

The portion of agency law relevant to this appeal is that which governs when the principal is liable to a third party for the actions of its agent. As a general rule, liability turns on whether the agent was acting with actual or apparent authority. Both types of authority depend on the acts of and communications by the principal. Actual authority turns on the reasonable belief of the *agent* based on such acts and communications. "An agent acts with actual authority when, at the time of taking action that has legal consequences for the principal, the agent reasonably believes, in accordance with the principal's manifestations to the agent, that the principal wishes the agent so to act." Restatement (Third) of Agency § 2.01. "An agent who has actual authority holds power as a result of a voluntary conferral by the principal and is privileged, in relation to the principal, to exercise that power." *Id.* § 1.01 cmt. c. Apparent authority, in contrast, turns on the reasonable belief of *a third party* based on the principal's acts and communications. "Apparent authority is the power held by an agent or other actor to affect a principal's legal relations with third parties when a third party reasonably believes the actor has authority to act on behalf of the principal and that belief is traceable to the principal's manifestations." *Id.* § 2.03.

An agent acting under actual or apparent authority can bind the principal to a contract with a third party. *See id.* § 6.01 . . . . The third party need not know the identity of the principal. *See id.* § 6.02 cmt. a (The principal is a party to a contract made by its authorized agent if the other party to the contract "has notice that the agent acts on behalf of a principal but does not have notice of the principal's identity."). And even if the agent does not disclose the existence of a principal, the principal will be a party to a contract made on its behalf by an agent acting with actual authority unless the contract specifically provides otherwise. *See id.* § 6.03. As the Restatement (Third) explains, "If an agent acts with actual authority in making a contract on an undisclosed principal's behalf, the basis for treating the principal as a party to the contract is that the agent acted reasonably on the basis of the principal's manifestation of assent to the agent. The principal's liability on the contract is thus consistent with the agent's reasonable understanding of the principal's wishes." *Id.* § 6.03 cmt. b (citations omitted); *see also San Juan Agr. Water Users Ass'n v. KNME-TV*, 150 N.M. 64, 257 P.3d 884, 889 (2011) ("An undisclosed principal can sue and be sued on a contract made in the agent's name because the common law of agency regards the agent's actions as the principal's own," as the agent's actions are "[u]nquestionably . . . in legal contemplation the acts of the principal" so long as they are within the agent's authority. (internal quotation marks omitted)).

The law governing the principal's liability for tort is a bit different, although there is overlap. As with liability on a contract, a principal is liable for tortious conduct of an agent when the conduct was within the scope of the agent's actual authority. *See* Restatement (Third) of Agency § 7.04(1). Thus, when an agent engages in tortious conduct that "the agent reasonably believes, on the basis of a manifestation of the principal," is in accordance with the principal's wishes, this conduct falls within the agent's actual authority and exposes the principal to liability in tort. *Id.* § 7.04 cmt. b.

But even when the agent's tortious act was not within the scope of the agent's actual authority, the principal may be liable under the doctrine of respondeat superior if the principal is the employer of the agent-employee and the tortious conduct was committed by the employee acting within the scope of employment. *Id.* § 7.07(1). For this purpose, we define *employee* as "an agent whose principal controls or has the right to control the manner and means of the agent's performance of work." *Id.* § 7.07(3)(a). (In the past an employee has also been referred to as a servant, and the principal has then been referred to as the master rather than the employer. *See* Restatement (Second) of Agency § 2 & cmt. a.)

What is very important, but often overlooked, is that not every agent is an employee. An agent who is not an employee is called an independent contractor, although some independent contractors (perhaps most) are not even agents. *See* Restatement (Third) of Agency § 1.01 cmt. c ("[T]he common term 'independent contractor' is equivocal in meaning and confusing in usage because some termed independent contractors are agents while others are nonagent service providers."). . . . (distinguishing between "employer-employee" and "independent-contractor" agency relationships).

The nature and extent of the principal's right to control the agent determines whether the agent is an employee or merely an independent contractor. To be sure, all agents are subject to the control of the principal; control is an essential element of the relationship. *See*

Restatement (Third) of Agency § 1.01 cmt. f(1) ("An essential element of agency is the principal's right to control the agent's actions.") . . . .

The right to control need not be exercised for an agency relationship to exist. It is the right of control, and not the actual exercise of control, that is an essential element of an agency relationship. "A principal's failure to exercise the right of control does not eliminate it . . . ." Restatement (Third) of Agency § 1.01 cmt. c. . . .

The principal's control may concern only the overall mission, not operational details. For instance, the principal may exercise control simply by giving initial instructions to the agent on what actions to take. "If the principal requests another to act on the principal's behalf, indicating that the action should be taken without further communication and the other consents so to act, an agency relationship exists." Restatement (Third) of Agency § 1.01 cmt. c; *see also id.* § 1.01 cmt. f(1) ("[W]ithin any relationship of agency the principal initially states what the agent shall and shall not do, in specific or general terms."). . . .

To be sure, as already suggested, "the principal retains the capacity throughout the relationship to assess the agent's performance, provide instructions to the agent, and terminate the agency relationship by revoking the agent's authority." Restatement (Third) of Agency § 1.01 cmt. f(1); *see id.* § 1.01 cmt. c . . .

But the critical point for our purposes is that, as the Restatement (Second) of Agency explains, the principal's "exercise [of control] may be very attenuated and, as where the principal is physically absent, may be ineffective." § 14 cmt. a; *see also United States v. Ackerman*, 831 F.3d 1292, 1301 (10th Cir. 2016) (Gorsuch, J.) ("[A] principal may delegate general authority to his or her agent to act in the ordinary course, without constant supervision or awareness of every discrete act."). . . .

This minimal level of control required to establish an agency relationship stands in contrast to the much more significant and intrusive right of control that makes an agent an employee. Recall how the Restatement (Third) defines *employee* for the purpose of applying respondeat superior: "an agent whose principal controls or has the right to control the manner and means of the agent's performance of work." § 7.07(3)(a); *see* § 7.07(1) (vicarious liability of employer for torts of employee). Implicit in this definition is that one can be an agent of a principal even if the principal does not control or have the right to control the "manner and means of the agent's performance of work." Otherwise, there would be no need for the definition in § 7.07(3)(a), as one could say simply that a principal is responsible for the tortious conduct of an agent committed while acting within the scope of the agency. In other words, although one requirement of an agency relationship is the principal's control or right of control over the agent, such control need not be control over the manner and means of the agent's performance of work; that higher level of control is necessary only to establish an employee relationship.

The Restatement (Third) does not explore in depth the meaning of "manner and means." But to determine whether to apply the doctrine of respondeat superior (that is, whether the principal is liable in tort), the New Mexico courts, following the guidance of the Restatement (Second), have frequently distinguished an employee from an independent contractor based on the power to control. They have said that "[a]n independent contractor is defined as 'a person who contracts with another to do something for him but who is not controlled by the other nor subject to the other's right to control with respect to his physical conduct in the performance of the undertaking.'" *Talbott v. Roswell Hosp. Corp.*, 138 N.M. 189, 118 P.3d 194, 197 (Ct. App. 2005) (quoting Restatement (Second) of Agency § 2(3)) (emphasis omitted); . . . But it must be recognized that the control of physical acts is not the exclusive consideration. New Mexico has "adopted the approach taken in the Restatement (Second) of Agency § 220, which incorporates many factors into the calculus of employee versus independent contractor." *Celaya v. Hall*, 135 N.M. 115, 85 P.3d 239, 243 (2004); *see id.* at 244 ("Applying all the factors in the Restatement to Defendant's job, and in light of the totality of the circumstances, we conclude that at the time of the incident Defendant undoubtedly was an employee of the Department. Considered in context, the Department exercised sufficient control over Defendant's activities in a manner consistent with the status of employee."). . . .

In short, where an agent does not need to be an employee to create liability for the principal—as when an agent with actual or apparent authority enters into a contract on the principal's behalf, *see* Restatement (Third) of Agency § 6.01—a minimal level of control may suffice. In particular, there is no requirement that the principal have the right to control the manner and means of the agent's performance of work. . . . The Second Circuit has succinctly stated the proposition: "Control is not a crucial question where the issue is liability for a contract . . . . If the agent had authority to enter into the contract, the principal will be bound." *Commercial Union Insurance Co. v. Alitalia Airlines*, 347 F.3d 448, 462 (2d Cir. 2003) . . .

2. Application

In concluding that Cervantes did not have the requisite right to control WKI's actions, the district court reasoned that WKI was an independent contractor because Cervantes "direct[ed] only the result to be accomplished, but not the manner in which it must be accomplished." *Alfaro-Huitron*, 2018 WL 522312, at *8 (applying New Mexico UJI 13–404, which defines *independent contractor* for purposes of respondeat superior). But this is the control test for the employer-employee relationship, not the lesser control necessary for an agency relationship. As the previous discussion explains, an independent contractor may be an agent even if it is not an employee, and a principal may be found responsible for an agent-independent contractor's contractual engagements even if it would not be liable for the contractor's torts. . . .

Applying the correct legal framework, we conclude that there is a genuine dispute of material fact about whether WKI acted as Cervantes's actual or apparent agent in recruiting Plaintiffs. Construing the factual record and the reasonable inferences to be drawn therefrom in the light most favorable to Plaintiffs, . . . we conclude that a jury could find that WKI and Plaintiffs had reasonable beliefs (traceable to manifestations by Cervantes) that Cervantes had authorized WKI to hire farmworkers for Cervantes. The reasonable belief by WKI establishes actual authority. *See* Restatement (Third) of Agency § 2.01. The reasonable belief by Plaintiffs establishes apparent authority. *See id.* § 2.03.

If Cervantes authorized WKI to hire workers for Cervantes through the H-2A program, it exercised all the control necessary to establish an agency relationship. "If the principal requests another to act on the principal's behalf, indicating that the action should be taken without further communication and the other consents so to act, an agency relationship exists." *Id.* § 1.01 cmt. c; Restatement (Second) of Agency § 14 cmt. a ("The right of control by the principal may be exercised by prescribing what the agent shall or shall not do before the agent acts, or at the time when he acts, or at both times.") . . . .

The Agreement executed by Dino Cervantes set forth the categories of workers ("skilled farm labor workers; U.S. Citizens, legal residents, or foreign workers with temporary working visas (H-2A)") as well as the type of work they would be performing, the number of workers, and the dates on which they would be working. Aplt. App., Vol. 3 at 474. WKI was required to submit the Agreement and other work contracts to the government to show that it had jobs available for the H-2A workers it sought, *see* 20 C.F.R. § 655.132(b)(4), and those contracts would have been meaningless if they did not create binding obligations on both the contractor and the farmer—particularly if they allowed a farmer to reject the contractor's recruitment of domestic workers at the wage rates required by the program. . . . Dino Cervantes testified that he knew WKI was submitting the Agreement to the DOL as a necessary part of its H-2A application and that H-2A workers would need to be paid the adverse-effect wage rate. A jury could find that it would have been reasonable for Mr. Campos to infer that he was authorized to hire workers for Cervantes, and that it would have been reasonable for those offered jobs by Mr. Campos (namely, Plaintiffs) to believe that WKI had that authority.

Although not essential to the conclusion that WKI was Cervantes's agent, we also note that the record supports the inference that Cervantes had the right to issue interim instructions to WKI: Mr. Campos testified that he would have followed any instructions that an agricultural business gave him regarding where he should recruit labor and that he would have had to replace any workers that a business did not want working on its farm. And Mr. Campos's conversations with the farm operators about the termination of their work agreements—including the message he left for Dino Cervantes on this topic—reflect his understanding that Cervantes and the other agricultural businesses had the power to revoke WKI's authority to recruit workers on their behalf, likewise demonstrating their right of control. *See* Restatement (Third) of Agency § 1.01 cmts. c and f(1); Restatement (Second) of Agency § 14 cmt. a.

Even if the level of control supported by the evidence was not "particularly invasive," . . . it was sufficient under New Mexico law to expose Cervantes to liability for WKI's alleged contractual breach. . . . We accordingly reverse the district court's grant of summary judgment in favor of Cervantes on Plaintiff's breach-of-contract claim and remand this claim for further proceedings. . . .

III. Conclusion

We REVERSE the district court's entry of summary judgment in favor of Cervantes on Plaintiffs' claims of breach of contract . . . and REMAND for further proceedings on those claims. . . .

CHAPTER 3

PARTNERSHIPS

2. THE LEGAL NATURE OF A PARTNERSHIP

Page 100. Insert the following at the bottom of the page:

The entity status can, however, be changed by the partnership agreement. *United States of America v. Sanofi Aventis U.S. LLC*, 226 A.3d 1117 (Del. 2020), held the Delaware version of the RUPA gives maximum effect to the freedom of contract so that the partnership agreement stating "the Partnership shall not be a separate legal entity distinct from its Partners" controlled the question before the court. The partnership was formed to pursue a *qui tam* action under the federal False Claims Act (FCA) against a drug company. After the suit was filed, one of the partners withdrew and was replaced by another person. Thereafter an amended complaint was filed on behalf of the new set of partners. The Delaware Supreme Court's ruling treated this as a new partnership, but more importantly held the partner's withdrawal caused the dissolution of the initial partnership, reasoning that the initial partnership was an association of its partners and not a distinct entity because the partnership agreement expressly stating that the partnership was an association and not an entity. The consequence of the dissolution meant that the pending *qui tam* action pursuant to the amended complaint must be dismissed—the FCA provides that once a *qui tam* action is filed (as it was with the original partnership) no private suit can thereafter be initiated. The court further held that the old partnership could not continue the pursue the *qui tam* action during its "winding up" process reasoning that the partnership's sole purpose was to pursue the *qui tam* action so that permitting the suit to be pursued would not be related to "liquidating" that partnership.

CHAPTER 4

The Foundations of a Corporation

9. Requisites for Valid Action by the Board

Page 268.* Insert the following before the first paragraph of text:

Bäcker v. Palisades Growth Capital II, L.P., 246 A.3d 81 (Del. 2021), adds further insight into the type of conduct that renders invalid action taken by directors. Alex Bäcker was the co-founder and majority common stockholder of QLess, Inc. (the "Company"). The Company also had outstanding two separate series of preferred shares—Series A and A-1, each series held by an institutional investor entitling each holder to elect one director.

Over many months, strained relations arose between Bäcker and the two institutional holders due to Bäcker's erratic and dictatorial management style that caused multiple operational problems at the firm. This prompted an internal investigation by an outside law firm into several workplace complaints. In response to the investigation's damning report, Bäcker initially fought hard to keep his role as CEO, but in June 2019 the Company's board removed Bäcker as CEO and appointed Kevin Grauman as his successor. Nonetheless, through control of the common stock held by Bäcker and his father, Bäcker continued to serve on the Company's board.

Grauman's appointment to the board was scheduled for the November 15, 2019, meeting. Also on that meeting's agenda was filling an existing vacancy associated with the Series A-1 Preferred Shares. In the week leading up to the meeting, the Company's outside counsel circulated board resolutions that, among other things, would appoint Grauman, then CEO, to the board, and fill the Series A-1 seat on the board. In the weeks leading up to that meeting, Bäcker made a series of statements that collectively represented his support for Grauman's appointment as CEO and that he should be a member of the board.

On the eve of the board meeting, the Company's independent director (a director selected by the combined voting of the common and preferred shares) unexpectedly resigned. This meant there were then only three directors—Bäcker, his father, and Anderson, the Series A Preferred designate. Bäcker leapt into action. He emailed those attending the board meeting (including the preferred's nominee to its vacant seat on the board) a bouncy message requesting that Grauman "distribute the board materials a day in advance of the meeting so that

---

*   Page 162 in the Concise Edition.

we may all do our homework and be prepared to spend our time together most productively." This email was seen by the courts as deceptively suggesting Bäcker's full concurrence with the agenda items, including Grauman's appointment to the board. The record clearly established that Bäcker planned to exploit the unexpected resignation to grab control of the board. Candor by Bäcker would have been fatal, because with there then being only three sitting directors Anderson could have barred any board action by not attending the meeting. But Anderson, believing the stars were aligned for a peaceful transfer of power, attended the meeting. At the meeting Bäcker move swiftly; with the support of his father, the board fired Grauman, appointed Bäcker CEO and CFO, expanded the board, added another ally to the board, and set the quorum at three thereby assuring a quorum would be met through the attendance of those aligned with Bäcker. The Vice-Chancellor referred to this as a *coup d'etat.*

On this record, the Delaware Supreme Court affirmed the Court of Chancery holding that Backer had committed deception in connection with the November meeting and on that finding imposed an equitable notice requirement for that meeting which was violated by Backer.

> This Court has long recognized that "inequitable action does not become permissible simply because it is legally possible."[120] Under Delaware law, "director action[s] [are] 'twice-tested,' first for legal authorization, and second [for] equity." . . .

> Consistent with these principles, Delaware courts have used their equitable powers on numerous occasions to invalidate otherwise lawful board actions tainted by inequitable deception. For example, in *Koch v. Stear*[,1992 WL 181717 (Del. Ch. July 28, 1992),] the court invalidated board actions terminating a CEO where a fellow director "tricked [the CEO] into attending the meeting" by circulating a special meeting notice that was "silent as to any possible consideration of" a transaction that would cause the board to remove the current CEO. . . .

> The Bäckers argue that the Court of Chancery's affirmative deception finding was clearly erroneous because the evidence does not show that the Bäckers falsely represented support for Grauman's appointment. . . .

> [T]he Court of Chancery identified at least one misrepresentation that passes muster . . . . On the day before the contested board meeting—and hours *after* Markman resigned—Bäcker asked Grauman to circulate board materials "so that *we* may all do *our* homework and be prepared to spend *our* time together most productively."

> This was an affirmative statement. Bäcker made the statement *after* Markman resigned. And the statement was

120   *Schnell v. Chris-Craft Indus., Inc.,* 285 A.2d 437, 439 (Del. 1971).

deceptive and misleading on its face. At that point, Bäcker knew that he held a board majority, and Bäcker had left Markman with the impression that he wanted to fire Grauman. Therefore, Bäcker must have known that the draft resolutions Alderton circulated earlier in the week were now a dead letter. Nonetheless, Bäcker asked that Grauman share his draft resolutions with Anderson and others "so that we may all do our homework." There was no reason for Grauman to prepare for a meeting from which he would be excluded and at which he would be fired. And there was no reason for Anderson or Grauman to study resolutions that Bäcker knew the board would not consider. It is not erroneous to find that this statement was deceptive. . . .

Thus, the Court of Chancery did not commit clear error by finding that the Bäckers deceived Anderson by falsely representing support for Grauman's appointment . . . .

[T]he Bäckers contend that the Court of Chancery erred by imposing an equitable notice requirement on a regular board meeting, contrary to this Court's holding in *Klassen*, which rejected a notice requirement for regular board meetings. . . .

. . . [T]he Court of Chancery never decided whether the November 15 Meeting was a regular meeting or a special one,[ ] and Alderton's minutes from the meeting "state[ ] that the Meeting was a special one." Regardless, the type of meeting is immaterial because the source of inequity is not the lack of notice, but the Bäckers' decision to secretly plan an ambush after feigning support for the planned governance items. Stated differently, contrary to the Bäckers' suggestion, the Court of Chancery did not impose an equitable notice requirement by faulting the Bäckers for staying silent. Instead, the court faulted the Bäckers for choosing to speak and mislead their fellow directors. Most notably, shortly before the November 15 board meeting Bäcker asked Grauman to "please distribute the board materials/deck a day in advance of the meeting so that we may all do our homework and be prepared to spend our time together most productively[.]"

This statement was deceptive. . . .

Nothing in . . . [Delaware] opinions suggest that Delaware law tolerates deception related to regular board meetings, and we can think of no good reason why deception would be allowed for regular board meetings, but forbidden for special board meetings.

Klassen does not save the Bäckers' argument. Contrary to the Bäckers' assertions, *Klassen* does not hold that equitable relief is unavailable where a director is tricked into attending a regular board meeting. Instead, the Court held more narrowly that because "[i]t is settled Delaware law that corporate directors are not required to be given notice of regular board meetings," the board's actions were not automatically invalid where the CEO-director "received no advance notice that his possible termination would be considered at that [regular board] meeting." Rejecting an advance notice requirement for regular board meetings did not grant parties a license to deceive. . . .

Regardless of the type of meeting or form of communications, Delaware law does not countenance deception designed to manufacture a quorum or otherwise induce director action.

Id. at 101–107.

15. THE OBJECTIVE AND CONDUCT OF THE CORPORATION

B. INTERESTS OTHER THAN MAXIMIZATION OF SHAREHOLDERS' WEALTH

Page 308.* Insert the following before the heading "Note on Benefit and Flexible Purpose Corporations":

NOTE ON THE SEC'S NEWLY-PROPOSED CLIMATE-RELATED DISCLOSURES

Millennials, more than prior generations, have expressed a keen interest in the social impact of their investments. The result, among others, has been a growing focus by institutional investors on how the activities of their portfolio companies affect the environment and, in turn, a demand for greater and more consistent climate-related disclosures.

The business community is facing a generational shift, from baby boomers to millennials. Over the next decade, millennials will assume a rising role among investors, employees, and consumers, and they will become the most dominant generation not long thereafter, outstripping their Generation X parents. . . .

Most relevant for our purposes, millennials are less focused on their investment returns than any generation since such questions were first asked. The evidence suggests not that they are indifferent to investment returns, but that they have a greater tendency to assess and even prioritize the social and other real world effects of their investments. Prior generations viewed larger social questions as belonging to the political sphere: the sphere of political campaigns, legislation, and perhaps litigation. The investment sphere was the place to make money and save for retirement. But millennial views

---

*   Page 196 in the Concise Edition.

and attitudes toward investment suggest a collapsing, or at least eroding, distinction between what were once thought of as distinct spheres of activity.

This broader, more socially conscious attitude toward investment is creating bottom-up pressure for investment funds to demonstrate how they advance socially important goals. That bottom-up pressure has now reached the upper-echelons of the market and is reshaping how these massively powerful institutional investors engage in activism. The reason why this bottom-up pressure has reached the upper echelons of the market is straightforward. The millennial generation will wield massive wealth and the race to manage that wealth has already begun.

The massive prize of managing millennial wealth has triggered a new high-stakes race among funds and has created strong competitive pressures to offer investment products that have high social value. . . .

Michal Barzuza, Quinn Curtis & David H. Webber, Shareholder Value(s): Index Fund ESG Activism and the New Millenial Corporate Governance, 83 S. Cal. L. Rev. 1243, 1284–85 (2020).

Reflecting investor concerns, on March 21, 2022, the Securities and Exchange Commission (SEC) formally launched one of the most significant initiatives in its nearly 90-year history: proposals for public disclosure of climate-related risks. (SEC, The Enhancement and Standardization of Climate-Related Disclosures for Investors, Rel. No. 33–11042 (Mar. 21, 2022)). Few firms, public or private, and certainly no investor, will be untouched by the forces unleashed by climate change. Thus, the historical significance of this SEC initiative is justified by the sheer enormity of climate-related risks and the diversity of forces underlying those risks.

Disclosure Requirements

The SEC proposals set forth numerous disclosure requirements that capture not just the uncertainty of how climate change might affect the firm, but also shine a light on management's strategies to cope with the potential tsunami. The new disclosures are to appear in SEC registration statements and annual reports.

Among the items required to be disclosed:

- The board's oversight and governance structure surrounding climate-related risks;

- The material impact(s) any climate-related risks have had or likely will have on the registrant's business and financial statements in the short-, medium-, and long-term;

- The registrant's climate-related targets or goals and any transition plan necessary to achieve them;

- The effect or likely effect of identified climate risks on the registrant's strategy, business model, and outlook;

- The registrant's process for identifying, assessing, and managing climate-related risks and whether this process is integrated into its risk management system; and

- The impact of climate-related events and transition activities on financial statement items as well as financial estimates (and related assumptions) that are affected by such climate-related events and transition activities.

Public companies will also be required to disclose their Scope 1 and Scope 2 greenhouse gas (GHG) emissions. Scope 1 covers direct GHG emissions from owned or controlled sources, and Scope 2 covers indirect GHG emissions from the generation of purchased electricity, steam, heating, and cooling consumed by the reporting company. Larger issuers, in addition, will be required to make disclosures relating to their Scope 3 emissions, which are indirect GHG emissions that occur in a company's value chain.

Do the Proposed Rules Exceed the SEC's Mandate?

If the new rules are adopted, challenges will include the claim that the proposals exceed the SEC's legislative authority and question whether there is sufficient evidence that the recommendations not only are "necessary or appropriate in the public interest" but also "will promote efficiency, competition, and capital formation," as articulated in the statement of the SEC's mission. *See, e.g.,* Securities Act of 1933 § 2(b).

In anticipation, the SEC's proposing release makes the case that disclosures of climate risk are well within the criteria the SEC draws upon when deciding mandatory disclosure requirements—namely, that the information enables investors to assess a firm's financial position, its operational performance, and management's stewardship, provided in a manner that facilitates comparisons among registrants. The release recognizes that climate risk is a broad concern among investors, who are eager to learn how companies might be or are being affected and how their management assesses those risks and plans to address them. This is very much within the SEC's lane.

The most novel of the mandated disclosures may be those for annual reporting of GHG emissions. The proposal provides that Scope 1 and Scope 2 disclosures will be required of all issuers. More challenging will be Scope 3 disclosures, as it requires disclosure related to GHGs produced by another entity outside the registrant's operational boundary. Of particular concern is that an issuer has a duty to disclose Scope 3 emissions if they are material. Thus, registrants will need to monitor their Scope 3 emissions to comply with the new disclosure requirements if their Scope 3 emissions rise to a material level. This part of the proposed disclosures raises an important question: Is it appropriate to mandate disclosure of information about operations that are beyond the registrant's governance boundaries? There is no doctrine in the securities laws, or with respect to materiality, that renders that kind of disclosure beyond the scope of the SEC's mandate. A focus on disclosing risk and enabling comparisons among investment opportunities should put a thumb on the scale in favor of the new Scope 3 requirements.

Corporate Governance Impact

As noted earlier, although the proposed rules do not mandate specific climate governance practices, they do require disclosures regarding the board's oversight and governance structure around climate-related risks. Those disclosures include:

- which directors have expertise in managing climate-related risks;
- which board committees have responsibility for climate oversight;
- the processes by which the board or board committees discuss climate risk and the frequency of those discussions;
- how the board or board committees integrate climate risk into the company's business strategy, risk management, and financial oversight; and
- how the board sets and oversees climate goals.

No doubt, the presence (or absence) of these practices will influence investor expectations and, in turn, influence how public companies manage their climate-related risks. The proposed rules may galvanize shareholder voting and activism, in particular as the new disclosures cause institutional shareholders and proxy advisory firms to focus more closely on board and management oversight. From that perspective, one might ask, to what extent are the new requirements crafted simply to inform investors of a company's climate-related risks, and to what extent are they likely to shape how those risks are governed and even the composition of the company's board and officers?

Many large institutional investors are already focused on the climate risk of their portfolio companies, and to that extent, the new rules may not significantly affect how those investors interact with the companies they invest in. Nevertheless, the new disclosures are in most cases more significant than what companies voluntarily disclose today, particularly with respect to GHGs. Public companies are likely to consider the potential effect of the new disclosures on stakeholders, in addition to the greater attention on climate-related governance that is likely to arise. In response, a public company may form a board committee, or expand the responsibilities of an existing committee, to include responsibility for oversight of climate-related risks and related disclosures (if they have not done so already). In line with the proposal's focus on climate-related expertise, the committee is likely to include one or more "climate risk experts," either at the board's prompting or in response to stakeholder demands. In addition, the new reporting requirements will require public companies to implement comprehensive procedures to manage the new disclosures. Those controls and procedures will include a management team (potentially under the oversight of a new C-suite manager) to oversee data collection and disclosure processes, new reporting systems, and checks-and-balances to verify data. And so, while the SEC's expressed focus is on enhancing climate-related risk disclosure, the proposed rules are also likely to affect how climate-related risks are managed if they are adopted.

CHAPTER 5

THE LEGAL STRUCTURE OF PUBLICLY HELD CORPORATIONS

1. THE LEGAL DISTRIBUTION OF POWER BETWEEN THE BOARD AND THE SHAREHOLDERS, AND EQUITABLE LIMITS ON THE BOARD'S LEGAL POWER

B. EQUITABLE LIMITS ON THE BOARD'S LEGAL POWERS

Page 334.* Insert the following after "Note on the Business Judgment Rule":

NOTE ON "ENTIRE FAIRNESS" STANDARD AND BLASIUS

In *Coster v. UIP Companies, Inc.*, 255 A.3d 952 (Del. 2021) (Seitz, C.J.), the Delaware Supreme Court determined that, even though the Chancery Court found a stock sale to have passed Delaware's rigorous "entire fairness" review, the court should have further considered whether the board acted for inequitable reasons or for the primary purpose of interfering with the stockholders' statutory or voting rights, including subjecting the board's actions to *Blasius*'s "compelling justification" standard of review. As the Supreme Court explained, " 'inequitable action does not become permissible simply because it is legally possible.' " The Supreme Court reasoned that if the board approved the stock sale for inequitable reasons, the Chancery Court should have canceled the stock sale. If the board, acting in good faith, approved the stock sale for the " 'primary purpose of thwarting' " the stockholder vote to elect directors or reduce the plaintiff's leverage as an equal stockholder, it must " 'demonstrat[e] a compelling justification for such action' " to withstand judicial scrutiny under *Blasius*.

Coster involved two equal stockholders of UIP Companies, Inc., a real estate investment services company, who were deadlocked and could not elect new directors. In light of the deadlock, one of the stockholders, Coster, sued for appointment of a custodian for UIP under Delaware General Corporation Law § 226(a)(1). In response, the three-person UIP board—comprised of the other equal stockholder and board chairman, Schwat, and two other directors aligned with him, Bonnell and Cox—voted to issue a one-third interest in UIP to Bonnell at a price based on a valuation that had been conducted by an independent financial advisor.

The Chancery Court concluded that the stock sale to Bonnell was motivated by a desire to dilute Coster's UIP ownership interest to below 50%,

---

*   Page 219 in the Concise Edition.

block her attempts to elect directors, and avoid a possible court-appointed custodian. The sale did just that. It likewise found that Schwat and Burnell were "interested" in the transaction, and thus the sale of stock to Bonnell was effected by a conflicted board. Consequently, the Chancery Court concluded, the defendant board had the burden of proving the entire fairness of the transaction.

Although the Chancery Court found that the "Stock Sale was significantly motivated by a desire to moot the Custodian Action" and the defendants "obviously desired to eliminate [Coster]'s ability to block stockholder action," it reasoned that "if the Stock Sale passed entire fairness review, the board's motives were 'beside the point.' " It determined that, although sub-optimal, the process employed by the UIP board was fair, especially in light of the directors' reliance on a third-party valuation. Having determined that the stock sale was entirely fair, the Chancery Court declined to appoint a custodian and dismissed Coster's action. In particular, the Chancery Court determined that, because the board had satisfied the rigorous "entire fairness" standard, it could not then proceed to scrutinize the transaction to determine, as urged by Coster, whether the board had a "compelling justification" to take the action it did in light of its impact on shareholder rights.

On appeal, the Delaware Supreme Court left undisturbed the Chancery Court's entire fairness determination. It did, however, find reversible error in the lower court's decision to limit its inquiry to entire fairness. The Supreme Court noted:

> In our view, the court bypassed a different and necessary judicial review where, as here, an interested board issues stock to interfere with corporate democracy and that stock issuance entrenches the existing board. As explained below, the court should have considered Coster's alternative arguments that the board approved the Stock Sale for inequitable reasons, or in good faith but for the primary purpose of interfering with Coster's voting rights and leverage as an equal stockholder without a compelling reason to do so.

> As early as *Schnell v. Chris-Craft Industries, Inc.,* we recognized that a board of directors could not escape judicial review of its actions by pointing to the legal authorization to undertake a given act. In *Schnell,* the incumbent board took admittedly legal action to move up the annual meeting date and change the location from New York City to a remote destination. These moves prevented a dissident slate from waging an effective election campaign. We held that the board's purposeful manipulation of the election machinery to entrench themselves violated the board's duty to act equitably toward stockholders. In a recent decision, we captured the essence of *Schnell* and the twice-tested judicial review of director action affecting the stockholder franchise:

>> This Court has long recognized that "inequitable action does not become permissible simply because it is legally possible."

Under Delaware law, "director action[s] [are] 'twice-tested,' first for legal authorization, and second [for] equity." "Stockholders can entrust directors with broad legal authority precisely because they know that that authority must be exercised consistently with equitable principles of fiduciary duty."

Delaware law recognizes that the stockholder franchise is the " 'ideological underpinning' upon which the legitimacy of the directors managerial power rests." Keeping "a proper balance in the allocation of power between the stockholders' right to elect directors and the board of directors' right to manage the corporation is dependent upon the stockholders' unimpeded right to vote effectively in an election of directors." "Accordingly, careful judicial scrutiny will be given [to] a situation in which the right to vote for the election of successor directors has been effectively frustrated and denied. . . ."

Delaware courts "have remained assiduous in carefully reviewing any board actions designed to interfere with or impede the effective exercise of corporate democracy by shareholders, especially in an election of directors." We have been clear that "where boards of directors deliberately employ[ ] various legal strategies either to frustrate or completely disenfranchise a shareholder vote. . . . [t]here can be no dispute that such conduct violates Delaware law." . . .

In *Canada Southern Oils, Ltd. v. Manabi Exploration Co., Inc.*, even though the corporation was in "dire financial plight," the court considered the circumstances surrounding the stock issuance and held that "the primary purpose behind the sale of these shares was to deprive plaintiff of the majority voting control" and enjoined the transaction. And in *Packer v. Yampol,* the court enjoined a preferred stock issuance meant to defeat a proxy contest. Although the company needed to raise capital, and raising capital might have been one purpose for issuing stock, "their primary purpose was to obstruct plaintiffs' ability to wage a meaningful proxy contest in order to maintain themselves in control."

Chancellor Allen summarized the import of these cases in *Glazer v. Zapata Corp.*:

> These cases stand for the proposition that directors may not act to frustrate the efforts of stockholders to elect new directors by engaging in transactions that are designed and pursued for the primary purpose of diluting the votes held by the insurgent stockholders. As such they are articulations of the principle which was old and well established when articulated in *Schnell v. Chris-Craft Industries*, . . . that "the subversion of corporate democracy by manipulation of corporate machinery will not be countenanced under Delaware law."

The Court of Chancery in *Blasius Industries, Inc. v. Atlas Corp.* held that, even though *Schnell* did not apply when the board acts in good faith, if the board nonetheless acts for the primary purpose of impeding stockholders' franchise rights, the board must prove a "compelling justification" for its actions. Our Court approved of the *Blasius* standard of review in *MM Cos., Inc. v. Liquid Audio, Inc.* . . . . We . . . explained in *Liquid Audio* that the board's actions "need not actually prevent the shareholders from attaining any success in seating one or more nominees in a contested election for directors and the election contest need not involve a challenge for outright control of the board of directors." Rather, to invoke *Blasius* the challenged board action "only need[s] to be taken for the primary purpose of interfering with or impeding the effectiveness of the stockholder vote in a contested election for directors."

Delaware courts will also closely scrutinize transactions that impede a stockholder's exercise of a statutory right relating to the election of directors. In *Phillips v. Insituform of North America, Inc.*, the Class B stockholders sought to enjoin a merger because the board issued new stock to deprive a receiver of the ability to act by written consent to replace the board. The court concluded that, when the corporation acts "solely or primarily for the express purpose" to deprive a stockholder of "effective enjoyment of a right conferred by law," "the board [must] demonstrate that the action taken was fair or justified given the particular business purpose sought to be achieved and the circumstances of the firm."

The Delaware Supreme Court concluded that the Chancery Court's finding of entire fairness did not substitute for further equitable review in light of Coster's allegations that an interested board approved the transaction to interfere with her voting rights and leverage as an equal stockholder. If the board had acted inequitably, it breached its fiduciary duty even if its actions were legal. And even where the board acted in good faith, "careful judicial scrutiny" was necessary where the stockholder franchise was frustrated or denied. As the Court concluded, notwithstanding a finding of entire fairness, the decision in *Blasius* makes clear that if the board acts with the "primary purpose" of interfering with a stockholder's statutory or voting rights, the board must "demonstrate a compelling justification" for its action to survive judicial scrutiny.

C. THE ROLE OF BYLAWS IN THE ALLOCATION OF POWER BETWEEN THE BOARD AND THE SHAREHOLDERS

Page 336.* Insert the following at the end of the carryover paragraph:

In *Strategic Investment Opportunities LLC v. Lee Enterprises, Inc.*, 2022 Del. Ch. LEXIS 34 (Del. Ch. Feb. 14, 2022), the Delaware Chancery

---

*   Page 221 in the Concise Edition.

Court upheld a board's rejection of a stockholder nomination notice due to the plaintiff's noncompliance with the unambiguous terms of the company's advance notice by-law. The stockholder's notice was not submitted by a record holder (in this case, plaintiff was the beneficial owner of shares held through The Depository Trust Company, whose nominee, and the shares' record holder, was Cede & Co., not the plaintiff) and information regarding the director nominees was not submitted on a form provided by the company, in each case as required by the company's by-law.

Strategic Investment Opportunities, when read with *Rosenbaum v. CytoDyn, Inc.*, 2021 WL 4775140 (Oct. 13, 2021), another recent Delaware Chancery Court decision upholding the rejection of stockholder nominees due to deficiencies in a stockholder notice, indicates that Delaware courts are likely to continue to enforce the specific terms of advance notice by-laws that are adopted on a "clear day" when there is no evidence that the board's actions were inequitable or manipulative.

The *Strategic Investment Opportunities* court applied an "enhanced scrutiny" standard of review in assessing the board's rejection of the nomination notice, requiring the directors to identify proper corporate objectives served by their actions and to justify their actions as reasonable in relation to those objectives. The court considered three key questions in its inquiry: whether the by-laws were clear and unambiguous (with any ambiguity resolved in favor of stockholders' electoral rights), whether the stockholder's nominations complied with the by-laws, and whether the company interfered with the plaintiff's attempt to comply.

Regarding the record holder requirement, the court found that the reason for it was "simple: the corporation wants to confirm that an individual or entity making proposals has 'skin in the game.'" Moreover, requiring director nominees to submit responses on a company-created questionnaire "furthers the information-gathering and disclosure functions of advance notice bylaws." And "[m]ore generally," the court found, "the Board had a genuine interest in enforcing its Bylaws so that they retain meaning and clear standards that stockholders must meet." Accordingly, finding the answer to the first key question to be "yes," and to the second and third key questions to be "no," the court denied plaintiff's request that its nominees be permitted to stand for election.

2. CORPORATE GOVERNANCE AND THE RISE OF INSTITUTIONAL SHAREHOLDERS

B. FINANCIAL INSTITUTIONS AND THEIR ADVISORS

Page 364. Insert the following at the end of note 8 "The Special Case of Mutual Funds":

Professors Bebchuk and Hirst's study the three major index fund managers—Black Rock, State Street and Vanguard—to conclude that, because the index fund's business model is premised on low operating costs fund managers have weak incentives to engage in monitoring the managers of portfolio firms'. *See* Index Funds and the Future of Corporate Governance: Theory, Evidence and Policy, 119 Colum. L. Rev. 2020, 2033–34 (2019). They support their thesis with data showing the Big Three do not engage managers on their operational issues; their engagement is rather focused on fairly-stylized guidelines they develop to identify governance practices, declassification of boards and majority vote provisions, they believe are otherwise well-received governance norms. Of note they find that the Big Three cast "no" advisory notes on CEO compensation one third as often as a cohort of ten active fund managers. *Id.* at 2090–93. On the other hand, Professors Barzuza, Curtis, and Webber in Shareholder Value(s): Index Fund ESG Activism and the New Millenial Corporate Governance, 93 S. Cal. L. Rev. 1243 (2020), find that index funds have been supportive of not only board diversity and corporate sustainability resolutions but also a broad range of ESG issues. They explain the funds' support of these issues because social issues are highly important to millennials who are a growing portion of the fund's targeted investors. Hence, an identity with ESG issues as very much platform of a fund's marketing itself to socially concerned investors as well as recruiting for its own workforce.

CHAPTER 6

SHAREHOLDER INFORMATIONAL RIGHTS & PROXY VOTING

1. SHAREHOLDER INFORMATION RIGHTS UNDER STATE AND FEDERAL LAW

A. INSPECTION OF BOOKS AND RECORDS

Page 404.* Insert the following after present note 6:

7. *Delaware's "Tools at Hand" Doctrine.* As will be studied later in Chapter 14, to survive a motion to dismiss a derivative suit, the plaintiff must allege specific facts to establish that a pre-suit demand on the board of directors is excused;[1] However, "[t]he law in Delaware is settled that plaintiffs in a derivative suit are not entitled to discovery to assist their compliance with the particularized pleading requirement of Rule 23.1 in a case of demand refusal." *Scattered Corp. v. Chi. Stock Exch., Inc.,* 701 A.2d 70, 77 (Del. 1997). Until this issue is resolved, the plaintiff is denied discovery to obtain the facts necessary to so plead. Similarly, discovery is not available in non-derivative shareholder suits until the complaint survives a motion to dismiss. Therefore, in shareholder suits in Delaware, absent access to company records and documents, when drafting the complaint the plaintiff's attorney is limited to information that is public, which is frequently less robust than the materials in the company's possession, so that the resulting complaint is less developed and likely not to survive a motion to dismiss.

However, the Delaware courts developed the "tools at hand" doctrine to balance the plaintiff's need for information to survive a motion to dismiss against the defendant's need to dispense with meritless suits at an early point in the litigation. The tools at hand doctrine encourages plaintiffs to use Section 220 (the right of inspection) to gather facts believed necessary to survive a motion to dismiss in shareholder litigation. The doctrine began with *Rales v. Blasband,* 634 A.2d 927, 934–35, n. 10 (Del. 1993), by the Delaware Supreme Court urging derivative plaintiffs to use Section 220 to access relevant corporate records for the purpose of fleshing out the

---

*   Page 284 in the Concise Edition.

1   See DEL. CH. CT. R. 23.1 ("In a derivative action . . . , the complaint shall allege . . . with particularity the efforts, if any, made by the plaintiff to obtain the action the plaintiff desires from the directors . . . and the reasons for the plaintiff's failure to obtain the action or for not making the effort."). This requires a plaintiff to show enough to create a reasonable doubt either that: (1) a majority of the board is independent for purposes of responding to the demand or refusing the demand; or (2) the challenged action is protected by the business judgment rule. *See Aronson v. Lewis,* 473 A.2d 805 (Del. 1984).

complaint so as to meet the particularization requirement to excuse a demand. *Aronson v. Lewis*, 473 A.2d 805, 814–15 (Del. 1984). Thus, *Rales* provided the basis for shareholders to employ Section 220 as a form of pre-suit discovery. A few years later, in *Grimes v. Donald*, 673 A.2d 1207 (Del. 1996), the court underscored the important function Section 220: "If the stockholder cannot plead such assertions consistent with Chancery Rule 11, after using the 'tools at hand' to obtain the necessary information before filing a derivative action, then the stockholder must make a pre-suit demand on the board." *Id.* at 1216. Since these decisions, plaintiffs in shareholder suits involving Delaware corporations have regularly initiated Section 220 requests as a prelude to pursuing a shareholder suit.

A recent study comparing litigated Section 220 requests maintained 1981–1994 with the post-*Rales* period 2004–2018, finds that post-*Rales* suits entail substantially more suits involving "books and records" requests than the previous norm of requests seeking a list of the shareholders and that many suits maintained after using the tools at hand yield outcomes favorable to plaintiffs. Moreover, the data supports the belief that such books and records litigation is something of a surrogate for a trial on the underlying claims of wrongdoing. *See*, James D. Cox, Kenneth J. Martin, and Randall S. Thomas, The Paradox of Delaware's "Tools at Hand" Doctrine: An Empirical Investigation, 75 Bus. Law. 2123 (2020).

———

Page 404.* Insert the following before "B. The Stockholder List in a Dematerialized World":

JUUL Labs, Inc. v. Grove
In the Court of Chancery of the State of Delaware, 2020.
2020 Del. Ch. Lexis 264.

Laster, V.C. Plaintiff JUUL Labs, Inc. (the "Company") is a privately held Delaware corporation with its principal place of business in San Francisco, California. Defendant Daniel Grove demanded to inspect books and records of the Company under Section 1601 of the California Corporations Code. *See* Cal. Corp. Code § 1601. That statute grants inspection rights to any stockholder in a corporation with its principal executive office in California, regardless of corporation's state of incorporation. Grove stated that he might sue in California state court to enforce his inspection rights.

The Company filed this action against Grove. . . . [T]he Company maintains that Grove cannot seek inspection under California law because, as a stockholder, he only can possess inspection rights under Section 220 of the Delaware General Corporation Law (the "DGCL"). *See* 8 *Del. C.* § 220. . . .

———

*   Page 284 in the Condensed Edition.

I.   Factual Background

Grove is a former employee of the Company. During his employment, Grove received options to acquire 20,000 shares of common stock as part of his compensation. . . .

On February 1, 2018, Grove exercised options to acquire 5,000 shares of common stock in the Company. . . .

On December 27, 2019, Grove demanded to inspect the books and records of the Company under Section 1601. Grove indicated that if he did not receive a response or if the Company refused his demand, then he "may apply to the [California state court] for an order compelling inspection." . . .

On January 6, 2020, the Company filed this action. The Company asked this court to enter an order

> . . . declaring that Delaware law (not California law) governs Grove's rights (if any) to inspect [the Company's] books and records; . . .

> . . . declaring that [the Company] is not obligated to make books and records available to Grove for inspection or otherwise. . . .

> . . . The parties cross-moved for judgment on the pleadings.

Meanwhile, on January 7, 2020, Grove filed an action in the Superior Court of California for the County of San Francisco. In the California action, Grove seeks to inspect the Company's books and records under Section 1601.

II.   Legal Analysis . . .

. . . The Internal Affairs Doctrine

The Company . . . argues that . . . [Grove] cannot pursue an inspection under [the California] statute because of the internal affairs doctrine. . . . Under the internal affairs doctrine as articulated by the Supreme Court of the United States and the Delaware Supreme Court, only Delaware law applies.

> The internal affairs doctrine is a conflict of laws principle which recognizes that only one State should have the authority to regulate a corporation's internal affairs—matters peculiar to the relationships among or between the corporation and its current officers, directors, and shareholders—because otherwise a corporation could be faced with conflicting demands.

Edgar v. MITE Corp., 457 U.S. 624, 645 (1982) (citing *Restatement (Second) of Conflict of Laws* § 302 cmt. b. (1971)). "Corporations are creatures of state law, and investors commit their funds to corporate directors on the understanding that, except where federal law expressly requires certain responsibilities of directors with respect to stockholders, state law will govern the internal affairs of the corporation." *Cort v. Ash*, 422 U.S. 66, 84 (1975), *abrogated on other grounds by Act Transamerica*

Mortg. Advisors, Inc. (TAMA) v. Lewis, 444 U.S. 11, 15 (1979). "No principle of corporation law and practice is more firmly established than a State's authority to regulate domestic corporations . . . ." *CTS Corp. v. Dynamics Corp. of Am.*, 481 U.S. 69, 89 (1987).

"[T]he internal affairs doctrine raises important Constitutional concerns—namely, under the Fourteenth Amendment Due Process Clause, the Full Faith and Credit Clause, and the Commerce Clause." *Salzberg v. Sciabacucchi*, 227 A.3d 102, 136 (Del. 2020). The Due Process Clause of the Fourteenth Amendment is implicated by the need for directors and officers "to know what law will be applied to their actions" and by the stockholders' "right to know by what standards of accountability they may hold those managing the corporation's business and affairs." *McDermott Inc. v. Lewis*, 531 A.2d 206, 216–17 (Del. 1987). The Full Faith and Credit Clause "commands application of the internal affairs doctrine except in the *rare* circumstance where national policy is outweighed by a significant interest of the forum state in the corporation and its shareholders." *Id.* at 218 (emphasis in original) (footnote omitted). Under the Commerce Clause, a non-chartering state " 'has no interest in regulating the internal affairs of foreign corporations.' " *Id.* at 217 (quoting *MITE*, 457 U.S. at 645–46); *accord Citigroup Inc. v. AHW Inv. P'ship*, 140 A.3d 1125, 1134 (Del. 2016) (explaining that when a claim implicates the internal affairs of a corporation, then "under the Commerce Clause and the Full Faith and Credit Clause, Delaware law would apply to the merits" (footnotes omitted)).

"The internal affairs doctrine applies to those matters that pertain to the relationships among or between the corporation and its officers, directors, and shareholders." *VantagePoint Venture P'rs 1996 v. Examen, Inc.*, 871 A.2d 1108, 1113 (Del. 2005). "The doctrine requires that the law of the state . . . of incorporation must govern those relationships." *Sagarra Inversiones, S.L. v. Cementos Portland Valderrivas, S.A.*, 34 A.3d 1074, 1082 (Del. 2011). Consequently, the "practice of both state and federal courts has consistently been to apply the law of the state of incorporation to the entire gamut of internal corporate affairs." *VantagePoint*, 871 A.2d at 1113 (internal quotation marks omitted). "The internal affairs doctrine," however, "does not apply where the rights of third parties external to the corporation are at issue, e.g., contracts and torts." *Id.* at 1113 n.14.

Stockholder inspection rights are a core matter of internal corporate affairs. In *Salzberg*, the Delaware Supreme Court constructed a Venn diagram depicting the extent to which issues potentially implicate internal affairs. 227 A.3d at 131. Within that Venn diagram, stockholder inspection rights occupy the innermost circle. Underscoring the centrality of stockholder inspection rights, the Delaware Supreme Court has described the ability of stockholders to access books and records as "an important part of the corporate governance landscape." *Seinfeld v. Verizon Commc'ns, Inc.*, 909 A.2d 117, 120 (Del. 2006) (internal quotation marks omitted). Through its Section 220 jurisprudence, the Delaware Supreme Court seeks to maintain "an appropriate balance" between the interests of stockholders to obtain information and the right of the corporation to deny unwarranted and burdensome requests. *Id.* at 118. The numerous Delaware decisions that address Section 220 rights demonstrate the significance of this subject as a matter of the internal affairs of Delaware corporations.

An important public policy served by the internal affairs doctrine is to ensure the uniform treatment of directors, officers, and stockholders across jurisdictions. "Uniform treatment of directors, officers and shareholders is an important objective which can only be attained by having the rights and liabilities of those persons with respect to the corporation governed by a single law." *Restatement (Second) of Conflict of Laws* § 302, cmt. e. "A State has an interest in promoting stable relationships among parties involved in the corporations it charters, as well as in ensuring that investors in such corporations have an effective voice in corporate affairs." *CTS Corp.,* 481 U.S. at 91. Having the law of the state of incorporation govern a corporation's internal affairs "prevent[s] corporations from being subjected to inconsistent legal standards" and "provide[s] certainty and predictability," thus "protect[ing] the justified expectations of the parties with interests in the corporation." *VantagePoint,* 871 A.2d at 1112–13.

Section 1601 is part of a suite of provisions in the California Corporations Code addressing information rights. Those provisions balance the relative interests of stockholders and the corporation differently than Section 220.

The core stockholder-inspection provision in the California regime appears in Section 1601(a) and states,

> The accounting books and records and minutes of proceedings of the shareholders and the board and committees of the board of any domestic corporation, *and of any foreign corporation keeping any such records in this state or having its principal executive office in this state,* shall be open to inspection upon the written demand on the corporation of any shareholder or holder of a voting trust certificate at any reasonable time during usual business hours, for a purpose reasonably related to such holder s interests as a shareholder or as the holder of such voting trust certificate. The right of inspection created by this subdivision shall extend to the records of each subsidiary of a corporation subject to this subdivision.

Cal. Corp. Code § 1601(a) (emphasis added). Although this provision generally resembles the right to inspect books and records granted by Section 220 of the DGCL, it differs in subtle ways. Most notably, the right to inspect "the records of each subsidiary" is broader than Section 220(b), which establishes a more limited right of access to a subsidiary's books and records. *See 8 Del. C.* § 220(b)(2). It also seems likely that there could be differences in judicial interpretation, although the parties have not highlighted them.

Related provisions address other aspects of California's information-rights regime. Section 1600 gives any stockholder holding at least 5% in the aggregate of the outstanding voting stock of a corporation or who holds at least 1% and has filed a proxy statement

> *an absolute right* to do either or both of the following: (1) inspect and copy the record of shareholders' names and addresses and shareholdings during usual business hours upon five business days' prior written demand upon the corporation, or (2) obtain from the transfer agent for the corporation, upon written demand and upon the tender of its usual charges for such a list (the amount of which charges shall be stated to the shareholder by the transfer agent upon request), a list of the shareholders' names and addresses, who are entitled to vote for the election of directors, and their shareholdings, as of the most recent record date for which it has been compiled or as of a date specified. . . . A corporation shall have the responsibility to cause its transfer agent to comply with this subdivision.

Cal. Corp. Code § 1600(a) (emphasis added). That section likewise "applies to any domestic corporation and to any foreign corporation having its principal executive office in this state or customarily holding meetings of its board in this state." *Id.* § 1600(d). Although the provision generally resembles the right to a stock list under Section 220 of the DGCL, a stockholder under Section 220(c)(3) is only *presumed* to have a proper purpose for obtaining a stock list, which shifts the burden to the corporation to show that the stockholder has an improper purpose. *See* 8 *Del. C.* § 220(c)(3). Under the California statute, the ability to access a stock list is an "absolute right." Cal. Corp. Code § 1600(a).

Section 1602 vests directors with "the absolute right at any reasonable time to inspect and copy all books, records and documents of every kind and to inspect the physical properties of the corporation of which such person is a director and also of its subsidiary corporations, domestic or foreign." Cal. Corp. Code § 1602. The inspection "may be made in person or by agent or attorney and the right of inspection includes the right to copy and make extracts." *Id.* The right "applies to a director of any foreign corporation having its principal executive office in this state or customarily holding meetings of its board in this state." *Id.* These provisions generally track a director's right to information under Section 220(d) and the common law interpreting it. Under Delaware law, however, a director's right to information is broad, but not absolute; a corporation can defeat the director's inspection right by showing that the director has an improper purpose. *See King v. DAG SPE Managing Member, Inc.*, 2013 WL 6870348, at *5 (Del. Ch. Dec. 23, 2013).

Sections 1603 and 1604 establish an enforcement regime. Section 1603(a) provides that a California state court in the proper county may enforce the right of inspection with just and proper conditions or may, for good cause shown, appoint one or more competent inspectors or accountants to audit the books and records kept in this state and investigate the property, funds and affairs of any domestic corporation or any foreign corporation keeping records in this state and of any subsidiary corporation thereof, domestic or foreign, keeping records in this state and to report thereon in such manner as the court may direct.

Cal. Corp. Code § 1603(a). Under the California statute, "[a]ll expenses of the investigation or audit shall be defrayed by the applicant unless the court orders them to be paid or shared by the corporation." *Id.* § 1603(c). The court may award legal fees and expenses to the applicant if the corporation's failure to comply with a proper demand was not substantially justified. *Id.* § 1604. Section 220 does not contain similar provisions, although this court has appointed receivers to enforce orders granting inspection rights. To obtain fee shifting under Delaware law, a stockholder must successfully invoke the bad faith exception to the American rule.

Generally speaking, the California inspection regime is not radically different from the Delaware regime, but it is not the same either. California's balancing of the competing interests between stockholders and the corporation differs from Delaware's. And California is not alone in granting rights to access the books and records of foreign corporations that do business in the state. If other states could define the terms by which stockholders can inspect books and records, then a Delaware corporation could be subjected to different provisions and standards in jurisdictions around the country.

Under constitutional principles outlined by the Supreme Court of the United States and under Delaware Supreme Court precedent, stockholder inspection rights are a matter of internal affairs. Grove's rights as a stockholder are governed by Delaware law, not by California law. Grove therefore cannot seek an inspection under Section 1601. . . .

III. Conclusion

. . . Under the internal affairs doctrine, . . . Grove does not have the right to seek an inspection of books and records under California law. That right exists only under Delaware law. . . .

2. THE PROXY RULES: AN INTRODUCTION

Page 422.* Insert the following to the end of note 4 *The "Universal Proxy"*:

In Securities Exchange Act Rel. No. 935596 (Nov. 17, 2021), the SEC adopted new Rule 14a–19 mandating the use of a universal proxy by all

---

*   Page 300 in the Concise Edition.

participants in director election contests. Thus, in future elections, all candidates will appear on the same proxy card so that in contested elections each party is to refer shareholders to the other party's proxy statement for information about the other party's nominees and explain that shareholders can access the other party's proxy statement without cost through the SEC's website. Among Rule 14a–19's requirements for the universal proxy are:

The universal proxy card must include the names of both registrant and dissident nominees, along with certain other shareholder nominees included as a result of proxy access;

Require dissidents to provide registrants with notice of their intent to solicit proxies and to provide the names of their nominees no later than 60 calendar days before the anniversary of the previous year's annual meeting;

Require registrants to notify dissidents of the names of the registrants' nominees no later than 50 calendar days before the anniversary of the previous year's annual meeting;

Require dissidents to file their definitive proxy statement by the later of 25 calendar days before the shareholder meeting or five calendar days after the registrant files its definitive proxy statement;

Require each side in a proxy contest to refer shareholders to the other party's proxy statement for information about the other party's nominees and refer shareholders to the SEC's website to access the other side's proxy statement free of charge;

Require that dissidents solicit the holders of shares representing at least 67% of the voting power of the shares entitled to vote at the meeting; and

Establish presentation and formatting requirements for universal proxy cards that ensure that each party's nominees are presented in a clear, neutral manner.

3.   THE PROXY RULES: SHAREHOLDER ACCESS

B.   SHAREHOLDER PROPOSALS UNDER RULE 14a–8

Page 428. Substitute the following for the first sentence of the paragraph after "B. Shareholder Proposals Under Rule 14a–8":

In 2020, the SEC amended Rule 14a–8 to change the required ownership threshold. There are now three alternative thresholds:

- $2,000 of the company's securities for at least three years;
- $15,000 of the company's securities for at least two years; or
- $25,000 of the company's securities for at least one year.

Page 429.* Add the following after "Note on No-Action Letters Interpreting Rule 14a–8":

The Artform of a Rule 14a–8 No-Action Letter: The Doris Behr 2012 Irrevocable Trust

Hal Scott, Trustee
Harvard Law School, Lewis 339, 1557 Massachusetts Ave,
Cambridge, MA 02138

November 9, 2018

Mr. Thomas J. Spellman III
Assistant General Counsel and
Corporate Secretary Johnson &
Johnson
One Johnson & Johnson Plaza
New Brunswick, NJ 08933

Dear Mr. Spellman:

The undersigned, as trustee of The Doris Behr 2012 Irrevocable Trust (the "Stockholder"), is providing this notice in accordance with Rule 14a–8 of the Securities Exchange Act of 1934, as amended ("Rule 14a–8"). The Stockholder offers the attached proposal (the "Proposal") for the consideration and vote of shareholders at the 2019 annual meeting of shareholders (the "Annual Meeting") of Johnson & Johnson (the "Company"). The Stockholder requests that the Company include the Proposal in the Company's proxy statement for the Annual Meeting.

Letters from the Stockholder's custodian and sub-custodian documenting the Stockholder's continuous ownership of the requisite amount of the Company's stock for at least one year prior to the date of this letter are attached. The Stockholder intends to continue its ownership of at least the minimum number of shares required by Rule 14a–8 through the date of the Annual Meeting.

I represent that the Stockholder or its agent intends to appear in person or by proxy at the Annual Meeting to present the attached Proposal.

Very truly yours,

Hal Scott Trustee
     Enclosures: Shareholder Proposal

---

*   Page 307 of the Condensed Edition.

Custodian and Sub-Custodian Letters

Resolved: The shareholders of Johnson & Johnson request the Board of Directors take all practicable steps to adopt a mandatory arbitration bylaw that provides:

- for disputes between a stockholder and the Corporation and/or its directors, officers or controlling persons relating to claims under federal securities laws in connection with the purchase or sale of any securities issued by the Corporation to be exclusively and finally settled by arbitration under the Commercial Rules of the American Arbitration Association (AAA), as supplemented by the Securities Arbitration Supplementary Procedures;

- that any disputes subject to arbitration may not be brought as a class and may not be consolidated or joined;

- an express submission to arbitration (which shall be treated as a written arbitration agreement) by each stockholder, the Corporation and its directors, officers, controlling persons and third parties consenting to be bound;

- unless the claim is determined by the arbitrator(s) to be frivolous, the Corporation shall pay the fees of the AAA and the arbitrator(s), and if the stockholder party is successful, the fees of its counsel;

- a waiver of any right under the laws of any jurisdiction to apply to any court of law or other judicial authority to determine any matter or to appeal or otherwise challenge the award, ruling or decision of the arbitrator(s);

- that governing law is federal law; and

- for a five-years unset provision, unless holders of a majority o Corporation shares vote for an extension and the duration of any extension.

Supporting Statement

The United States is the only developed country in which stockholders of public companies can form a class and sue their own company for violations of securities laws. As a result, U.S. public companies are exposed to litigation risk that, in aggregate, can cost billions of dollars annually. The costs (in dollars and management time) of defending and settling these lawsuits are borne by stockholders. Across the corporate landscape, this effectively recirculates money within the same investor base, minus substantial attorneys' fees. Lawsuits are commonly filed soon after merger or acquisition announcements, or stock price changes, based on little more than their happening. We believe arbitration is an effective alternative to class actions. It can balance the interests and rights of plaintiffs to bring federal securities law claims, with cost-effective protections for the corporation and its stockholders.

The Supreme Court has held that mandatory individual arbitration provisions are not in conflict with any provision of the federal securities laws, and the SEC has no basis to prohibit mandatory arbitration provisions that apply to federal securities law claims. Furthermore, New Jersey law establishes that the bylaws of a corporation are to be interpreted as a contract between the corporation and its stockholders.

A bylaw providing for mandatory individual arbitration of federal securities law claims would permit stockholders and corporations to opt-out of a flawed system that often seems more about the lawyers than the claimants and invariably wastes stockholder funds on expensive litigation costs.

Skadden, Arps, Slate, Meagher & Flom LLP

1440 New York Avenue, N.W. Washington, D.C. 20005–2111
TEL: (202)371-7000
FAX: (202)393-5760
www.skadden.com

FIRM/AFFILIATE OFFICES

———————

BOSTON CHICAGO HOUSTON LOS ANGELES NEW YORK
PALO ALTO WILMINGTON

———————

BEIJING BRUSSELS

marc.gerber@skadden.com

BY EMAIL (shareholderproposals@sec.gov)

FRANKFURT
HONG KONG
LONDON
MOSCOW
MUNICH
PARIS
SÃO PAULO
SEOUL
SHANGHAI
SINGAPORE
TOKYO
TORONTO

January 16, 2019

U.S. Securities and Exchange Commission Division of
Corporation Finance
Office of Chief Counsel 100 F Street,
N.E. Washington, D.C.20549

> RE: Johnson & Johnson—2019 Annual
> Meeting Supplement to Letter dated
> December 11, 2018 Relating to
> Shareholder Proposal of The Doris Behr
> 2012 Irrevocable Trust

Ladies and Gentlemen:

We refer to our letter dated December 11, 2018 (the "No-Action Request"), submitted on behalf of our client, Johnson & Johnson, a New Jersey corporation, pursuant to which we requested that the Staff of the Division of Corporation Finance (the "Staff") of the U.S. Securities and Exchange Commission (the "Commission") concur with Johnson & Johnson's view that the shareholder proposal and supporting statement (the "Proposal") submitted by The Doris Behr 2012 Irrevocable Trust (the "Proponent") may be excluded from the proxy materials to be distributed by Johnson & Johnson in connection with its 2019 annual meeting of shareholders (the "2019 proxy materials").

This letter supplements the No-Action Request. In accordance with Rule 14a–8(j), we are simultaneously sending a copy of this letter and its attachment to the Proponent.

I. The Proposal May be Excluded Pursuant to Rule 14a–8(i)(2) Because Implementation of the Proposal Would Cause Johnson & Johnson to Violate State Law.

As described in the No-Action Request, Rule 14a–8(i)(2) permits a company to exclude a shareholder proposal if implementation of the proposal would cause the company to violate any state, federal or foreign law to which it is subject. For the reasons described below and based upon the legal opinion of Lowenstein Sandler LLP, attached hereto as Exhibit A (the "New Jersey Opinion"), Johnson & Johnson believes that implementation of the Proposal would cause Johnson & Johnson to violate New Jersey law. Accordingly, the Proposal is excludable under Rule 14a–8(i)(2) as a violation of law.

Johnson & Johnson is incorporated in the State of New Jersey and, as explained in both the No-Action Request and the New Jersey Opinion, adoption of a bylaw amendment requested by the Proposal would prohibit any shareholder from bringing claims arising under the federal securities laws in connection with the purchase or sale of any securities issued by Johnson & Johnson in court (including New Jersey courts) and instead require such persons to arbitrate such claims. For the reasons provided in the New Jersey Opinion, Johnson & Johnson believes that adoption of a bylaw amendment as described in the Proposal violates New Jersey law and that adoption of such a bylaw amendment would be subject to legal challenges. Johnson & Johnson believes that it should not be required to include a proposal to adopt such a bylaw amendment in the 2019 proxy materials where the bylaw amendment requested would, if adopted, likely be the subject of costly litigation. Furthermore, even if the Staff believes that the legality of the bylaw amendment requested by the Proposal is an open question, the Staff has previously concurred with the exclusion of shareholder proposals to amend a company's bylaws under Rule 14a–8(c)(1), the predecessor to Rule 14a–8(i)(1), a sister rule to Rule 14a–8(i)(2), where the Staff found that the proposed bylaw amendments were of "questionable validity." *See Radiation Care, Inc.* (Dec. 22, 1994) (permitting exclusion under Rule 14a–8(c)(1) of a proposal to amend the bylaws to, among other things, authorize the expenditure of corporate funds effected by shareholders without any concurring action by the board of directors, noting that even if the proposal were recast in precatory terms, it would nevertheless constitute an improper subject for shareholder action because the proposal contained a provision of questionable validity under Delaware law) and *Pennzoil Corp.* (Feb. 24, 1993, recon. denied, Mar. 22, 1993) (same).

As more fully described in the New Jersey Opinion, a New Jersey corporation's bylaws may not contain a provision that is inconsistent with law, and the New Jersey Opinion expresses the view that a New Jersey court, if presented the question, would likely conclude that New Jersey corporations may not lawfully mandate arbitration in their constitutive documents as the forum to resolve claims of shareholders for alleged violations of the federal securities laws. In addition, a New Jersey court presented with the question would likely conclude that shareholders who did not approve an arbitration provision in a New Jersey corporation's bylaws would not have provided the mutual assent required to enforce an arbitration agreement, as determined under customary principles of contract law, such that a mandatory arbitration bylaw would likely be held inconsistent with New Jersey law and, therefore, invalid. Accordingly, Johnson & Johnson believes that implementation of the Proposal would violate New Jersey law.

On numerous occasions, the Staff, pursuant to Rule 14a–8(i)(2), has permitted exclusion of shareholder proposals regarding bylaw amendments (either mandatory amendments or precatory proposals) that, if implemented, would cause the company to violate state law. *See, e.g., Vail Resorts, Inc.* (Sept. 16, 2011) (permitting exclusion under Rule 14a–8(i)(2) of a proposal to amend the bylaws to "make distributions to shareholders a higher priority than debt repayment or asset acquisition" because the proposal would cause the company to violate state law); *Citigroup, Inc.* (Feb. 18, 2009) (permitting exclusion under Rule 14a–8(i)(2) of a proposal to amend the bylaws to establish a board committee on U.S. economic security because the proposal would cause the company to violate state law); *Monsanto Co.* (Nov. 7, 2008, recon. denied, Dec. 18, 2008) (permitting exclusion under Rule 14a–8(i)(2) of a proposal to amend the bylaws to require directors to take an oath of allegiance to the U.S. Constitution because the proposal would cause the company to violate state law); *Hewlett-Packard Co.* (Jan. 6, 2005) (permitting exclusion under Rule 14a–8(i)(2) of a proposal recommending that the company amend its bylaws so that no officer may receive annual compensation in excess of certain limits without approval by a vote of "the majority of the stockholders" because the proposal would cause the company to violate state law).

Finally, as noted in the New Jersey Opinion, Johnson & Johnson acknowledges that no New Jersey court has considered the issue of whether a mandatory arbitration bylaw requiring shareholders to arbitrate claims under the federal securities laws would be legal as a matter of New Jersey law. However, as is typically the case, the New Jersey Opinion uses legal reasoning from existing New Jersey statutes and case law, and analogizes to case law from Delaware and the U.S. Court of Appeals for the Third Circuit, to come to an opinion as to how a New Jersey court would likely view a novel question presented by adoption of a bylaw amendment as described in the Proposal. The Staff has previously allowed for the exclusion of shareholder proposals pursuant to Rule 14a–8(i)(2) where there was no case law directly on point. *See General Motors Corp.* (Apr. 19, 2007) (permitting exclusion under Rule 14a–8(i)(2) of a proposal requiring directors to oversee certain functional groups excludable even though the company's Delaware counsel expressly noted that there was "no Delaware case that specifically addresses the validity of the Proposed Bylaw or a similar bylaw"); *Citigroup Inc.*(Feb. 18, 2009) (permitting exclusion under Rule 14a–8(i)(2) of a proposal to amend the bylaws to establish a board committee on U.S. economic security excludable where the proponent argued that, because there had not been a court decision regarding the matters addressed in the Delaware law opinion related to the no-action request, the Staff should not grant no-action relief to the company).

Accordingly, consistent with the precedent described above, Johnson & Johnson believes the Proposal should be excluded from the 2019 proxy materials pursuant to Rule 14a–8(i)(2) because implementation of the Proposal would cause Johnson & Johnson to violate state law.

II. Conclusion

For the reasons stated above and in the No-Action Request, Johnson & Johnson respectfully requests that the Staff concur that it will take no action if Johnson & Johnson excludes the Proposal from the 2019 proxy materials.

Should the Staff disagree with the conclusions set forth in this letter, or should any additional information be desired in support of Johnson & Johnson's position, we would appreciate the opportunity to confer with the Staff concerning these matters prior to the issuance of the Staffs response. Please do not hesitate to contact the undersigned at (202) 371-7233.

Very truly yours,

Marc S. Gerber

UNITED STATES
SECURITIES AND EXCHANGE COMMISSION
WASHINGTON, D.C. 20549

DIVISION OF
CORPORATION FINANCE

February 11, 2019

Marc S. Gerber
Skadden, Arps, Slate, Meagher & Flom LLP
marc.gerber@skadden.com

Re: Johnson & Johnson

Incoming letter dated December 11, 2018

Dear Mr. Gerber:

This letter is in response to your correspondence dated December 11, 2018 and January 16, 2019 concerning the shareholder proposal (the "Proposal") submitted to Johnson & Johnson (the "Company") by The Doris Behr 2012 Irrevocable Trust (the "Proponent") for inclusion in the Company's proxy materials for its upcoming annual meeting of security holders. We have received correspondence on the Proponent's behalf dated December 24, 2018, January 23, 2019 and February 1, 2019. We also have received correspondence from the Attorney General of the State of New Jersey dated January 29, 2019. Copies of all of the correspondence on which this response is based will be made available on our website at http://www.sec.gov/divisions/corpfin/cf-noaction/14a-8.shtml. For your reference, a brief discussion of the Division's informal procedures regarding shareholder proposals is also available at the same website address.

Sincerely,

M. Hughes Bates Special Counsel

Enclosure

cc: Hal Scott

The Doris Behr 2012 Irrevocable Trust hscott@law.harvard.edu

February 11, 2019

Response of the Office of Chief Counsel Division of Corporation Finance

Re: Johnson & Johnson

Incoming letter dated December 11, 2018

The Proposal requests that the board take all practicable steps to adopt a bylaw provision to require disputes between a shareholder and the Company, its directors, officers or controlling persons relating to certain claims under the federal securities laws to be exclusively and finally settled by arbitration.

The Company requested that the staff concur in the Company's view that it may exclude the Proposal from its 2019 proxy materials pursuant to rule 14a–8(i)(2), which permits a company to exclude a shareholder proposal "[i]f the proposal would, if implemented, cause the company to violate any state, federal, or foreign law to which it is subject." The Company argued that the Proposal would cause the Company to violate federal and state law.

As to state law, the Company argued that implementation of the Proposal would cause the Company to violate the state law of New Jersey, where it is incorporated, and provided a New Jersey legality opinion from counsel supporting its view. The Proponent raised arguments in rebuttal. We carefully considered the parties' submissions.

When parties in a rule 14a–8(i)(2) matter have differing views about the application of state law, we consider authoritative views expressed by state officials. Here, the Attorney General of the State of New Jersey, the state's chief legal officer, wrote a letter to the Division stating that "the Proposal, if adopted, would cause Johnson & Johnson to violate New Jersey state law." We view this submission as a legally authoritative statement that we are not in a position to question.

In light of the submissions before us, including in particular the opinion of the Attorney General of the State of New Jersey that implementation of the Proposal would cause the Company to violate state law, we will not recommend enforcement action to the Commission if the Company omits the Proposal from its proxy materials in reliance on rule 14a–8(i)(2). To conclude otherwise would put the Company in a position of taking actions that the chief legal officer of its state of incorporation has determined to be illegal. In granting the no-action request, the staff is recognizing the legal authority of the Attorney General of the State of New Jersey; it is not expressing its own view on the correct interpretation of New Jersey law. The staff is not "approving" or "disapproving" the substance of the Proposal or opining on the legality of it. Parties could seek a more definitive determination from a court of competent jurisdiction.

We are also not expressing a view as to whether the Proposal, if implemented, would cause the Company to violate federal law. Chairman Clayton has stated that questions regarding the federal legality or regulatory implications of mandatory arbitration provisions relating to claims arising under the federal securities laws should be addressed by the Commission in a measured and deliberative manner.

Sincerely,

Jacqueline Kaufman Attorney-Adviser

Page 437.* Substitute the following for the note material immediately following *Trinity Wall St. v. Wal-Mart Stores, Inc.*:

SEC, Division of Corporation Finance, Shareholder Proposals: Staff Legal Bulletin No. 14L (Nov. 3, 2021).

This bulletin outlines the Division's views on Rule 14a–8(i)(7), the ordinary business exception, and Rule 14a–8(i)(5), the economic relevance exception. . . . In addition, we are providing new guidance on the use of e-mail for submission of proposals, delivery of notice of defects, and responses to those notices.

In Rule 14a–8, the Commission has provided a means by which shareholders can present proposals for the shareholders' consideration in the company's proxy statement. This process has become a cornerstone of shareholder engagement on important matters. Rule 14a–8 sets forth several bases for exclusion of such proposals. Companies often request assurance that the staff will not recommend enforcement action if they omit a proposal based on one of these exclusions ("no-action relief"). The Division is issuing this bulletin to streamline and simplify our process for reviewing no-action requests, and to clarify the standards staff will apply when evaluating these requests. . . .

Rule 14a–8(i)(7), the ordinary business exception, is one of the substantive bases for exclusion of a shareholder proposal in Rule 14a–8. It permits a company to exclude a proposal that "deals with a matter relating to the company's ordinary business operations." The purpose of the exception is "to confine the resolution of ordinary business problems to management and the board of directors, since it is impracticable for shareholders to decide how to solve such problems at an annual shareholders meeting."[1] . . .

Based on a review of . . . [the staff's experiences in guidance], we recognize that an undue emphasis was placed on evaluating the significance of a policy issue to a particular company at the expense of whether the proposal focuses on a significant social policy, complicating the application of Commission policy to proposals. In particular, we have found that focusing on the significance of a policy issue to a particular company has drawn the staff into factual considerations that do not advance the policy objectives behind the ordinary business exception. We have also concluded that such analysis did not yield consistent, predictable results.

Going forward, the staff will realign its approach for determining whether a proposal relates to "ordinary business" with the standard the Commission initially articulated in 1976, which provided an exception for certain proposals that raise significant social policy issues[3] . . . . This exception is

---

*   Page 307 in the Concise Edition replacing the note devoted to SEC Staff Legal Bulletin 14H.

[1]   Release No. 34–40018 (May 21, 1998) (the "1998 Release"). Stated a bit differently, the Commission has explained that "[t]he 'ordinary business' exclusion is based in part on state corporate law establishing spheres of authority for the board of directors on one hand, and the company's shareholders on the other." Release No. 34–39093 (Sept. 18, 1997).

[3]   Release No. 34–12999 (Nov. 22, 1976) (the "1976 Release") (stating, in part, "proposals of that nature [relating to the economic and safety considerations of a nuclear power plant], as

essential for preserving shareholders' right to bring important issues before other shareholders by means of the company's proxy statement, while also recognizing the board's authority over most day-to-day business matters. For these reasons, staff will no longer focus on determining the nexus between a policy issue and the company, but will instead focus on the social policy significance of the issue that is the subject of the shareholder proposal. In making this determination, the staff will consider whether the proposal raises issues with a broad societal impact, such that they transcend the ordinary business of the company. . . .

Rule 14a–8(i)(5), the "economic relevance" exception, permits a company to exclude a proposal that "relates to operations which account for less than 5 percent of the company's total assets at the end of its most recent fiscal year, and for less than 5 percent of its net earnings and gross sales for its most recent fiscal year, and is not otherwise significantly related to the company's business."

Based on a review of . . . staff experience applying the guidance . . . we believe . . . [that] proposals that raise issues of broad social or ethical concern related to the company's business may not be excluded, even if the relevant business falls below the economic thresholds of Rule 14a–8(i)(5). . . .

Page 442. Insert the following at the top of the page:

NOTE ON CONTRASTING PROPOSALS BY GADFLIES WITH THOSE BY FINANCIAL INSTITUTIONS

Nickolay Gantchev and Mariassunta Giannetti, The Costs and Benefits of Shareholder Democracy: Gadflies and Low-Cost Activism, 34 Rev. of Fin. Studies 5629 (2021), examines 4,878 shareholder proposals between 2003 and 2014. They find that firms targeted by individuals do not differ in any meaningful way from firms targeted by institutions as firms are all relatively large and have reported low profitability. About 20 percent of the proposals voted on garnered a majority or greater vote, with individuals the most frequent proponents accounting for over 35 percent of all proposals voted on at meetings. Proposals submitted by individuals were more likely to be approved than those submitted by institutions.[2] Moreover, they find concentration of submitted proposals is higher among individuals than among institutions—the top three individuals account for about 50% of all individual proposals, whereas the top three institutions account for about 30% of all institutional proposals. They report that on average in a given year the top individual proponent submits 52 proposals compared to 44 by the top union proponent and 38 by the top pension proponent. Proposals by mutual funds are negligible in number.

---

well as others that have major implications, will in the future be considered beyond the realm of an issuer's ordinary business operations").

[2]   There is a conflict in the studies over whether proposals submitted by individuals are more likely to pass than proposals submitted by institutions. Compare Gillan and Starks (2000) (proposals sponsored by individuals less likely to pass) with Gantchev and Giannetti (2020) (shareholder proposals by individuals more likely to pass). The sample period for Gillan and Starks is much earlier than that of the other study suggesting a change in behavior may have occurred over time.

The study's authors document that a small group of individuals, often referred to as corporate gadflies, submits a disproportionate number of proposals. These individual sponsors, such as John Chevedden and William Steiner, do not acquire large stakes and are not particularly wealthy, but submit dozens of shareholder proposals every year. However, proposals by such active individuals receive the lowest percentage of votes across a range of types of proposals and only are implemented by boards 3% of the time, whereas overall the implementation rate for majority-passed proposals is 12%.[3] The study's authors believe the gadflies poor success are is because their proposals are not tailored to the conditions that surround the targeted firm; this weakness is understood by the stockholders. They also find that "proposals implemented by active individual sponsors [i.e. gadflies] destroy shareholder value if they are implemented."

---

[3]   Id. at 17. The authors argue that even this small percentage of proposals destroy value when they are implemented, but that boards do so because they fear "the personal consequences arising from ISS withhold vote recommendations, which are typically issued when majority supported proposals are not implemented, regardless of their quality." Id. at 2.

CHAPTER 7

Personal Liability in a Corporate Context

3. Veil Piercing

Add to page 484.* Insert after "Berle, The Theory of Enterprise Entity":

Lynn M. Lopucki, The Essential Structure of Judgment Proofing
51 Stan. L. Rev. 147, 156–158 (1998).

On what principle could a court collapse . . . [two cooperating entities] into one?

The principle most often suggested is "enterprise." That is, the court should determine the scope of the business enterprise and collapse all of the "constituent parts . . . functioning as an integral part of a united endeavor" into one. Phillip I. Blumberg, The Law of Corporate Groups: Problems in the Bankruptcy or Reorganization of Parent and Subsidiary Corporations, § 1.03 at 10 (1985). The problem with that approach is that the boundaries of the modern enterprise are ethereal and transitory. . . .

To illustrate the problem a court could face in determining the boundaries of an enterprise without reference to its form, consider the example of an $80 million judgment for food poisoning at a hypothetical fast-food restaurant franchise. The negligent employees were employed by Franchisee, Inc. Under the doctrine of respondeat superior, that corporation is liable, but it owns nothing. The land and building are owned by and leased from a Real Estate Investment Trust (REIT) that owns hundreds of such properties. The equipment in the restaurant is owned by and leased from a national leasing company. The trademark and business systems are owned by the franchisor, Franchisor, Inc. The franchise agreement provides that the franchise is not property and that Franchisor, Inc. can cancel it at any time, with or without cause.

. . . Holding the franchisee's enterprise to own all assets indispensable to the business adds nothing. Regardless of the type of asset considered, some businesses operate without owning it, or at least without having any equity in it. For example, many businesses lease the real estate they occupy and the equipment they use. A decision to include in the enterprise all the assets *used* in the business would create more problems than it would solve. For instance, airports are used in the

---

* Page 351 before Note on an Empirical Analysis of Piercing Cases in Condensed Edition.

businesses of airlines, but no one advocates permitting judgment creditors of a bankrupt airline to levy on those airports and collect from them. One may be tempted to say that the airport is outside the enterprise because it is used by several businesses. Yet to limit the "enterprise" to assets *used exclusively* by the business would give up too much. Under this regime, the debtor could shield assets, such as aircraft, simply by sharing use with another airline.

———

Page 501.* Insert the following before "Note on Variations Among States in Applying the Piercing-the-Veil Doctrine":

Manichaean Capital, LLC v. Exela Technologies, Inc.

Court of Chancery of Delaware, 2021.
251 A.3d 694.

[As studied later in this casebook, Delaware and other state corporate statutes provide an appraisal proceeding whereby shareholders can receive in cash the fair value of their shares if they believe the consideration offered in a merger is not sufficient. Manichaean Capital had obtained a significant appraisal award in connection with the merger of SourceHOV Holdings into what became Exela Technologies. Following final judgment, to facilitate payment, the Chancery Court entered a charging order against SourceHOV Holdings' interests in its subsidiaries, but the judgment remained unsatisfied. The charging order required any money flowing through SourceHOV Holdings first to be paid to plaintiffs. In other words, to the extent Exela, as parent of SourceHOV Holdings, wished to receive distributions from its subsidiaries below SourceHOV Holdings, any money that flowed through SourceHOV Holdings should first be paid to plaintiffs before reaching Exela. Plaintiffs alleged that Exela and its subsidiaries abused the corporate form through fraudulent maneuvers to prevent funds that would otherwise flow from SourceHOV Holdings' subsidiaries directly to SourceHOV Holdings to bypass SourceHOV Holdings and flow instead directly to Exela. It did so through a $160 million accounts receivable securitization facility ("A/R Facility") through which SourceHOV Holdings' subsidiaries sold their accounts receivable to Exela subsidiaries which, in turn, used those receivables as collateral for loans and letters of credit. The A/R Facility permitted value once held by SourceHOV Holdings' subsidiaries to be held by an Exela subsidiary, allowing a diversion of funds around SourceHOV Holdings and directly to Exela. Plaintiffs therefore sought to pierce the corporate veil upwards to reach Exela and downwards (*i.e.*, reverse veil-piercing) from

———

*   Page 351 in Condensed Edition.

SourceHOV Holdings to its wholly-owned subsidiaries, which plaintiffs alleged were complicit in abusing the corporate form.]

The question of whether and to what extent courts of Delaware should allow so-called reverse veil-piercing is one of first impression. This is not to say that parties in litigation have not asked our courts to authorize reverse veil-piercing. They have. But our courts have yet to accept or deny the claim. For reasons explained below, I am satisfied that Delaware law allows for reverse veil-piercing in limited circumstances and in circumscribed execution.

At its most basic level, reverse veil-piercing involves the imposition of liability on a business organization for the liabilities of its owners. . . . As the doctrine has evolved, courts now recognize two variants of reverse veil-piercing: insider and outsider reverse veil-piercing. Insider reverse veil-piercing is implicated where "the controlling [member] urges the court to disregard the corporate entity that otherwise separates the [member] from the corporation." Outsider reverse veil-piercing is implicated where "an outside third party, frequently a creditor, urges a court to render a company liable on a judgment against its member." Given Plaintiffs are creditors of SourceHOV Holdings, the single member and 100% owner of SourceHOV LLC, which in turn is the single member and owner of the SourceHOV Subsidiaries, and Plaintiffs seek to hold the subsidiaries liable for a judgment held against the member, this case concerns outsider veil-piercing.

The case associated with the first substantive treatment of reverse veil-piercing is Judge Learned Hand's decision in *Kingston Dry Dock Co. v. Lake Champlain Transp. Co.* There, the court considered a trial court order allowing a judgment creditor to seize property of a subsidiary controlled by the judgment debtor in satisfaction of the judgment. In refreshingly short order, Judge Hand found that reverse veil-piercing was not warranted. In doing so, he observed that the subsidiary had not "interpose[d] in any way in the conduct of [the parent's] affairs." He also emphasized that "[s]o long as the law allows associated groups to maintain an independent unity, its sanction is not so easily evaded, and persons dealing with either do so upon the faith of the undertaking of that one which they may select." And so began the reverse veil-piercing debate. Since then, many courts have adopted the doctrine, while others have shied away.

Courts declining to allow reverse veil-piercing have relied primarily, and understandably, on a desire to protect innocent parties. . . .

The concerns . . . are well-founded. To start, reverse veil-piercing has the potential to bypass normal judgement collection procedures by permitting the judgment creditor of a parent to jump in front of the subsidiary's creditors. For obvious reasons, this dynamic would "unsettle the expectations of corporate creditors who understand their loans to be secured . . . by corporate assets" and could lead to corporate creditors "insist[ing] on being compensated for the increased risk of default posed by outside reverse-piercing claims." As (if not more) important, "to the extent that the corporation has other non-culpable shareholders, they obviously will be prejudiced if the corporation's assets can be attached directly." Courts rejecting reverse veil-piercing have emphasized that the risk of harm to innocent stakeholders is often avoidable because judgment creditors can invoke other claims and remedies to achieve the same outcome.

The risks that reverse veil-piercing may be used as a blunt instrument to harm innocent parties, and to disrupt the expectations of arms-length bargaining, while real, do not, in my view, justify the rejection of reverse veil-piercing outright. . . .

In *C.F. Trust, Inc. v. First Flight L.P.*, the Supreme Court of Virginia . . . recognized the risk that reverse veil-piercing could negatively impact innocent third-parties and defined the reverse veil-piercing standard expressly to manage that risk. Specifically, the court held that a plaintiff asking the court to authorize reverse veil-piercing, in addition to proving the elements required to justify traditional veil-piercing, must also demonstrate that reverse veil-piercing will not cause harm to "innocent investors . . . [or] innocent secured and unsecured creditors," and that there are no other legal or equitable remedies "availab[le] . . . [for] the creditor [to] pursue."

Similarly, in *In re Phillips*, the Supreme Court of Colorado . . . clarified that, in evaluating reverse veil-piercing claims, courts must first make the traditional determinations of whether the subsidiary is an alter ego of the parent and whether the subsidiary is being used in perpetration of fraud or injustice. Then the court must assess whether there is an inequitable result that can be remedied by piercing. And finally, before authorizing the piercing, the court must consider whether innocent shareholders or creditors would be prejudiced as a result of the piercing.

In the only case cited by the parties that purported to apply Delaware law, [*Sky Cable, LLC v. DIRECTV, Inc.*, 886 F.3d 375 (4th Cir. 2018)], the court likewise acknowledged the risks of reverse veil-piercing and then addressed how limits on the doctrine would adequately manage those risks. As with other courts that have adopted reverse veil-piercing, the Fourth Circuit found it difficult to justify an outright rejection of the doctrine when "the same considerations that justify [traditional] piercing [of] the corporate veil" are at work to justify a plaintiff's request to "pierc[e] the veil in reverse." In the traditional veil-piercing context, Delaware courts have forcefully stated that "Delaware has a powerful interest of its own in preventing the entities that it charters from being used as vehicles for fraud. Delaware's legitimacy as a chartering jurisdiction depends on it." With this in mind, the *Sky Cable* court noted that if reverse veil-piercing was not available, such that an alter ego entity could not be held liable for its member's debts under any circumstance, "fraudulent members could hide assets in plain sight to avoid paying a judgment." To address this unacceptable outcome, the court held that where: (1) an LLC has a single member, (2) that LLC is the member's alter ego, and (3) that member is using the LLC as a fraudulent shield against judgment creditors, reverse veil-piercing is a tool available to the court to avoid fraud and injustice when other legal and equitable means are unavailing.

. . . I am satisfied there is a place for a carefully circumscribed reverse veil-piercing rule within Delaware law.

In defining the rule, I begin by stressing that I am not endorsing "insider" reverse veil-piercing. The rule stated here applies only to "outsider" reverse veil-piercing. Also at the threshold, it must be emphasized that, just like with traditional veil-piercing, reverse veil-piercing should be sanctioned only in the most "exceptional circumstances." The framework outlined here to evaluate reverse veil-piercing claims comes with an express recognition that such claims, if not guided by appropriate standards, can threaten innocent third-party creditors and shareholders and lead to a host of unpredictable outcomes for these constituencies. Only in cases alleging egregious facts, coupled with the lack of real and substantial prejudice to third parties, should the court even consider utilizing the reverse veil-piercing doctrine. With prejudice to third-parties in mind and a framework designed to deal with such concerns, however, reverse veil-piercing can act as a deterrent to owners of companies, particularly those that are closely held, from shuffling their assets among their controlled entities with the express purpose of avoiding a judgment.

The natural starting place when reviewing a claim for reverse veil-piercing are the traditional factors Delaware courts consider when reviewing a traditional veil-piercing claim—the so-called "alter ego" factors that include insolvency, undercapitalization, commingling of corporate and personal funds, the absence of corporate formalities, and whether the subsidiary is simply a facade for the owner. The court should then ask whether the owner is utilizing the corporate form to perpetuate fraud or an injustice. This inquiry should focus on additional factors, including "(1) the degree to which allowing a reverse pierce would impair the legitimate expectations of any adversely affected shareholders who are not responsible for the conduct of the insider that gave rise to the reverse pierce claim, and the degree to which allowing a reverse pierce would establish a precedent troubling to shareholders generally; (2) the degree to which the corporate entity whose disregard is sought has exercised dominion and control over the insider who is subject to the claim by the party seeking a reverse pierce; (3) the degree to which the injury alleged by the person seeking a reverse pierce is related to the corporate entity's dominion and control of the insider, or to that person's reasonable reliance upon a lack of separate entity status between the insider and the corporate entity; (4) the degree to which the public convenience, as articulated by [the Delaware General Corporation Law and Delaware's common law], would be served by allowing a reverse pierce; (5) the extent and severity of the wrongful conduct, if any, engaged in by the corporate entity whose disregard is sought by the insider; (6) the possibility that the person seeking the reverse pierce is himself guilty of wrongful conduct sufficient to bar him from obtaining equitable relief"; (7) the extent to which the reverse pierce will harm innocent third-party creditors of the entity the plaintiff seeks to reach; and (8) the extent to which other claims or remedies are practically available to the creditor at law or in equity to recover the debt. Fundamentally, reverse veil-piercing, like traditional veil-piercing, is rooted in equity, and the court must consider all relevant factors, including those just noted, to reach an equitable result.

Applying this framework, Delaware courts will be well-equipped to handle the varying concerns courts and commentators have rightfully expressed regarding reverse veil-piercing. The expectations of third-party creditors and investors will be well-protected. And the "public convenience" factor will require "the balancing of the social value of upholding the legitimate expectations of the affected corporate creditors or debtors, applying a rebuttable presumption in favor of assuring such expectations, against the importance of the policies served by allowing a reverse pierce under the particular circumstances involved."

... It is at least reasonably conceivable that the SourceHOV Subsidiaries are alter egos of SourceHOV Holdings and that the subsidiaries have actively participated in a scheme to defraud or work an injustice against SourceHOV Holdings creditors, like Plaintiffs, by diverting funds that would normally flow to SourceHOV Holdings away from that entity to Exela. At this stage, from the well pled allegations in the Complaint, I see no innocent shareholders or creditors of the SourceHOV Subsidiaries that would be harmed by reverse veil-piercing, nor any potential alternative claims at law or in equity, as against the SourceHOV Subsidiaries or SourceHOV Holdings itself, that would for certain remedy the harm.

[Accordingly, the *Chancery Court* denied the motion to dismiss claims based on plaintiffs' reverse veil-piercing theories.]

———

The next case concerns a limited liability company (LLC). Even though generally speaking LLCs are the subject of Chapter 9, the principles adopted in the case apply fully as well to piercing in a corporate context.

Sky Cable, LLC v. DIRECTV, Inc.

United States Court of Appeals for the Fourth Circuit, 2018.
886 F.3d 375.

■ **Judges:** Before KEENAN, WYNN, and HARRIS, CIRCUIT JUDGES. JUDGE KEENAN wrote the opinion, in which JUDGE WYNN and JUDGE HARRIS joined.

■ BARBARA MILANO KEENAN, CIRCUIT JUDGE.

In 2013, the district court held Randy Coley (Mr. Coley) liable for conducting a fraudulent scheme involving the unauthorized transmission of television programming provided by DIRECTV, LLC (DIRECTV). The court entered judgment against Mr. Coley in the amount of over $2.3 million. After an unsuccessful attempt to satisfy its judgment against Mr. Coley personally, DIRECTV filed a motion in the district court to "reverse pierce" the "corporate veil" of three of Mr. Coley's limited liability companies (LLCs), contending that the three entities were "alter egos" of Mr. Coley. The district court granted DIRECTV's motion, finding that the LLCs were alter egos of Mr. Coley and, thus, were subject to execution of DIRECTV's judgment against Mr. Coley.

This appeal raises the question whether application of Delaware law in this case permits the remedy of reverse piercing a corporate veil of an LLC, when the LLC has been determined to be the alter ego of its sole member. Upon our review, we affirm the district court's decision to allow this remedy, based on our consideration of existing Delaware law and of the overwhelming evidence that the LLCs at issue were alter egos of Mr. Coley. . . .

I.

Randy Coley has operated various businesses that provide consumers access to cable television services. DIRECTV widely distributes cable television services to many entities and individuals, including services to facilities that have multiple residential rooms, such as hotels and hospitals. In 2000, Mr. Coley, through his now-defunct company East Coast Cablevision, LLC (ECC), contracted with DIRECTV to provide its programming to 168 rooms at the Massanutten Resort in Virginia. By May 2011, Mr. Coley was receiving payment for cable services provided to over 2,500 units at Massanutten by DIRECTV. During this time, however, Mr. Coley continued to pay DIRECTV only for services provided to the original 168 units, and fraudulently retained the excess revenue received for services provided to more than 2,300 units. Mr. Coley and ECC continued to provide unauthorized DIRECTV programming to those additional units at the Massanutten Resort until DIRECTV initiated an investigation and discovered the fraudulent scheme.

In 2011, Sky Cable, LLC (Sky Cable), a dealer of DIRECTV's services, sued Mr. Coley . . . and DIRECTV, among others, in the district court, alleging that Sky Cable had been deprived of certain revenue as a result of Mr. Coley's unlawful distribution scheme at the Massanutten Resort. The court ultimately dismissed Sky Cable's claims against DIRECTV, but DIRECTV filed cross-claims in the case under 47 U.S.C. § 605(a) against Mr. Coley . . . and ECC for unauthorized receipt and distribution of DIRECTV's programming.

The evidence before the district court showed that in addition to ECC, Mr. Coley also managed three other LLCs, namely, Its Thundertime, LLC (ITT), East Coast Sales, LLC (East Coast), and South Raleigh Air, LLC (South Raleigh). At issue in this case is appellant ITT, an LLC in which Mr. Coley is the sole member, which was incorporated in 2008 under Delaware law. Mr. Coley stated that he created ITT to hold title to real property for various rental properties purchased by him and his wife. According to Mr. Coley, ITT collected only the profit, as opposed to the entire revenue, obtained from rentals of these properties. DIRECTV has not alleged that ITT was a part of the illegal cable television transmission scheme conducted by Mr. Coley and ECC.

The evidence further showed that Mr. Coley is also the sole member of East Coast and South Raleigh, each of which manages and collects income on the properties owned by ITT. Mr. Coley and these three LLCs have engaged in a continuous commingling of funds. For example, on various occasions, Mr. Coley directed that one LLC transfer funds to another LLC to pay certain expenses, including mortgage payments on properties for which Mr. Coley and his wife were the mortgagors. Mr. Coley at times also admitted that he did not keep complete records of how and why funds were transferred between him and his LLCs. . . .

After years of litigation, the district court entered judgment in favor of DIRECTV against Mr. Coley and ECC for certain violations of federal communications law under 47 U.S.C. § 605(a). The court awarded damages to DIRECTV in the amount of $2,393,000. . . .

DIRECTV was unable to collect any payment on the judgment from Mr. Coley, who allegedly has few personal assets. Mr. Coley apparently dissolved ECC after the district court entered its judgment. However, discovery in the case revealed that several of Mr. Coley's LLCs, including ITT, held title to or managed Mr. Coley's assets. Therefore, to enforce its judgment against Mr. Coley, DIRECTV filed a motion in the district court to reverse pierce the corporate veil of ITT, East Coast, and South Raleigh to obtain access to the LLCs' assets. These three LLCs were not parties to the case and had not been served with process. . . .

[T]he district court entered an amended judgment rendering the three LLCs co-judgment debtors with Mr. Coley. The district court held that: (1) under Delaware law, the three LLCs were alter egos of Mr. Coley, and (2) that Delaware would recognize reverse veil piercing under such circumstances. . . .

III.

A.

Mr. Coley and ITT (the defendants) contend that the district court erred in reverse piercing ITT's corporate veil. They primarily assert . . . that Delaware law does not permit reverse piercing of a corporate veil, even when the corporation is an alter ego of the judgment debtor . . . .

In response, DIRECTV argues that the district court correctly predicted that Delaware law would permit reverse veil piercing under these factual circumstances . . . .

Like a corporation, an LLC also generally protects its "members" from personal liability for the LLC's debts. *See NetJets Aviation, Inc. v. LHC Commc'ns, LLC*, 537 F.3d 168, 176 (2d Cir. 2008).

Nevertheless, courts have disregarded the legal distinction between a business entity and the individuals who hold ownership interests in that entity, if maintaining the distinction would "produce injustices or inequitable consequences." *DeWitt*, 540 F.2d at 683 (citation omitted). In such circumstances, a court may "pierce the veil" separating the entity and its constituent members and treat the entity and its members as identical. *See id.* Importantly, similar circumstances warrant piercing the veil of both corporations and LLCs. *NetJets*, 537 F.3d at 176.

Traditional veil piercing permits a court to render an individual liable in a judgment against a business entity in which the individual has an interest, when the entity "is in fact a mere instrumentality or alter ego of [the individual]." *Id.* . . . Conversely, reverse veil piercing attaches liability to the *entity* for a judgment against the individuals who hold an ownership interest in that entity. *See C.F. Tr., Inc. v. First Flight, L.P.*, 306 F.3d 126, 134 (4th Cir. 2002) (explaining that reverse piercing renders the entity liable for debts of a member). . . .

Reverse piercing is classified into two types, namely, insider reverse piercing and outsider reverse piercing. . . . "Insider" reverse piercing applies when "the controlling [member or shareholder] urges the court to disregard the corporate entity that otherwise separates the [member or shareholder] from the corporation." 1 James D. Cox & Thomas Lee Hazen, *Treatise on the Law of Corporations* § 7:18 [Cox & Hazen] (3d ed. 2017). However, many courts strongly oppose allowing a company's veil to be pierced for the benefit of the individuals who themselves have created the company. . . .[6] "Outsider" reverse piercing, the type relevant here, applies when an outside third party, frequently a creditor, urges a court to render a company liable in a judgment against its member. *First Flight*, 306 F.3d at 134 ("Outsider reverse veil-piercing extends [the] traditional veil-piercing doctrine to permit a third-party creditor to 'pierce[ ] the veil' to satisfy the debts of an *individual* out of the corporation's assets." (citation omitted and second alteration in original)).

---

[6] Because insider reverse piercing is not at issue in this case, we express no opinion on the propriety of that theory under Delaware law.

Many courts have allowed outsider reverse piercing in actions by creditors, Cox & Hazen, *supra*, § 7:18, because outsider reverse piercing "follows logically the premises of traditional veil piercing," O'Neal & Thompson, *supra*, § 8:18. The states that have barred outsider reverse piercing have done so "in large part because of the potential harm to innocent shareholders [or members]."[7] Cox & Hazen, *supra*, § 7:18. . . .

Although there are obvious differences between piercing an entity's veil to render an individual liable, and piercing the veil to render a company liable, we have explained that in many jurisdictions "the same considerations that justify [traditional] piercing [of] the corporate veil may justify piercing the veil in 'reverse.'" *First Flight*, 306 F.3d at 135 (citing 1 *Fletcher, supra*, § 41.70). . . . Notably, in Delaware, disregarding the corporate fiction "*can always be done* if necessary to prevent fraud or chicanery," a principle that would support both traditional and reverse veil piercing. . . . Just as traditional veil piercing permits a court to hold a member liable for a company's actions, reverse veil piercing permits a court to hold a company liable for a member's actions if recognizing the corporate form would cause fraud or similar injustice. *See Pauley*, 239 A.2d at 633; *Harco Nat'l Ins. Co. v. Green Farms, Inc.*, No. CIV. A. 1131, 1989 Del. Ch. LEXIS 114, 1989 WL 110537, at *4 (Del. Ch. Sept. 19, 1989). . . .

Reverse veil piercing is particularly appropriate when an LLC has a single member, because this circumstance alleviates any concern regarding the effect of veil piercing on other members who may have an interest in the assets of an LLC. *See* 1 *Fletcher, supra*, § 41.70 (noting that "potential harm" to other members "must be considered"). Therefore, when an entity and its sole member are alter egos, the rationale supporting reverse veil piercing is especially strong. . . .

We also observe that "Delaware has a powerful interest of its own in preventing the entities that it charters from being used as vehicles for fraud. Delaware's legitimacy as a chartering jurisdiction depends on it." *NACCO Indus., Inc. v. Applica Inc.*, 997 A.2d 1, 26 (Del. Ch. 2009). Were Delaware to permit courts to hold an alter ego member liable for an entity's debts *without also* allowing courts to hold the alter ego entity liable for the member's debts, fraudulent members could hide assets in plain sight to avoid paying a judgment. . . .

And finally, Delaware courts have signaled some willingness to apply a theory of reverse veil piercing. In *Spring Real Estate, LLC v. Echo/RT Holdings, LLC*, the Court of Chancery of Delaware noted that "where [a] subsidiary is a mere alter ego of the parent to the extent that the Court may engage in 'reverse veil-piercing,' the Court may treat the assets of the subsidiary as those of the parent" for certain purposes. No.

---

[7]   Many other states have recognized the remedy of reverse piercing in certain circumstances. *See First Flight*, 306 F.3d at 135 (collecting cases from various jurisdictions).

CV 7994-VCN, 2016 Del. Ch. LEXIS 46, 2016 WL 769586, at *3 (Del. Ch. Feb. 18, 2016). . . .

B.

Mr. Coley next argues that the district court erred in concluding that ITT was his alter ego. He contends that such a conclusion required the court to find that ITT had a fraudulent purpose. Mr. Coley asserts that because the court failed to make a finding of fraudulent purpose, the court erred in reverse piercing ITT's veil. We disagree with Mr. Coley's argument. . . .

If legally separate entities fail to follow corporate formalities when doing business with one another, this failure may raise an inference that the entities are one and the same.[11] *See NetJets*, 537 F.3d at 178. Additionally, piercing an entity's veil under the alter ego theory is particularly appropriate when a single individual or entity completely dominates and controls another entity. *Wallace*, 752 A.2d at 1183–84.

Here, the district court found that ITT, East Coast, and South Raleigh were Mr. Coley's alter egos because they "operate as a single economic entity in which money flows freely between them at [Mr.] Coley's whim." The court further found significant evidence of "[Mr.] Coley's failure to observe corporate formalities, an utter lack of proper accounting records, and extensive commingling of assets." We conclude that the district court did not clearly err in its alter ego finding.

We reject Mr. Coley's contention that an alter ego must have been created with an expressly fraudulent purpose. *See NetJets*, 537 F.3d at 177 (noting that there is no requirement that an alter ego was "originally intended to perpetrate a fraud" (citing *Martin*, 88 A. at 615)). Instead, it is enough that the entity was used to cause fraud or injustice. *See id.* at 176–77; *Pauley*, 239 A.2d at 633; *Harco*, 1989 Del. Ch. LEXIS 114, 1989 WL 110537, at *5.

The evidence that Mr. Coley and his LLCs are alter egos is substantial. Mr. Coley clearly controls ITT and, on multiple occasions, testified pre-judgment that he is ITT's sole member. Mrs. Coley separately testified that she had no ownership interest in any of Mr. Coley's business entities and was not a member of ITT. Mr. Coley also produced an operating agreement during pre-judgment discovery listing himself as ITT's only member, and testified that he is the only one who "get[s] a check" from his LLCs.

There is also abundant evidence in the record that Mr. Coley and his LLCs commingled their funds. Mr. Coley failed to keep complete records of how and why funds were deposited from one LLC's account into another LLC's account, or into his personal accounts. Checks made out to "East Coast Sales" were sometimes deposited into Mr. Coley's personal

---

[11]   LLCs must observe fewer *internal* formalities than corporations, but the principle that they should follow ordinary formalities and norms when doing business with other entities is the same. *NetJets*, 537 F.3d at 178.

account. However, Mr. Coley also received income directly from East Coast. Mr. Coley even reported East Coast's profit and loss on his individual tax return. Yet, in his deposition testimony, Mr. Coley could not explain the amounts that he received from his LLCs as salary and other income. For example, he stated as follows:

> Q: Well, I'm trying to understand, Mr. Coley, what do you exactly buy with your own money. Because as far as I can tell, you've got at least $130,000 flowing into your and [Mrs. Coley's] account, your tax return from 2014 reports business income of $66,000 and a bunch of losses. And so I'm trying to understand how that all fits together. Can you explain it to me?

> A: No. I don't know how—I don't—I can't explain this here. I can't explain that.

Funds also were transferred freely among the LLCs. For example, South Raleigh and East Coast collected the rental revenue on properties owned by ITT, but South Raleigh and East Coast then transferred that revenue, less their expenses, to ITT as profit. Mr. Coley failed to explain why the revenue did not go directly to ITT, the owner of the properties. And when asked why certain transfers of funds also were made *from* ITT to one of the other LLCs, Mr. Coley had no explanation. . . .

Finally, the LLCs also made payments on mortgages for properties owned by ITT. Mr. Coley testified that on one such property, East Coast made payments on the mortgage loan, but that he and his wife were the borrowers. South Raleigh also made mortgage payments on a separate property owned by ITT, for which Mr. and Mrs. Coley were the borrowers. Moreover, even the mortgage on Mr. Coley's personal residence was paid by one of his LLCs. Nevertheless, Mr. Coley took the mortgage interest deduction on such properties on his *personal* tax return. This cumulative evidence strongly indicates that Mr. Coley and his LLCs were in fact a single economic entity, *NetJets*, 537 F.3d at 176, utterly dominated and controlled by Mr. Coley, *Wallace*, 752 A.2d at 1183. We also conclude that an "overall element of injustice or unfairness" is present in this case, because DIRECTV has not received any payment on its judgment against Mr. Coley although the district court found Mr. Coley liable over four years ago. *See NetJets*, 537 F.3d at 176.

We therefore hold that the district court's finding that ITT and Mr. Coley are alter egos was not clearly erroneous. . . .

CHAPTER 9

LIMITED LIABILITY COMPANIES

1. INTRODUCTION: FORMATION AND MANAGEMENT OF LLCS

Page 658.* Add the following immediately after conclusion of "*4. Members' Interest*":

5. *The Corporate Transparency Act.* In 2021 Congress enacted the Corporate Transparency Act. The Act requires non-exempt limited liability companies and corporations to file a report containing the names, dates of birth, addresses, and unique identification numbers (for example, the number on a passport or a driver's license) of the company's beneficial owners. The Report is to be filed with the Financial Crimes Enforcement Network (FinCEN), a bureau of the United States Treasury Department.

A beneficial owner is defined to mean a person who directly or indirectly exercises substantial control over a corporation or a limited liability company, owns 25% more of the equity interests in a corporation or a limited liability company, or receives substantial economic benefits from the assets of a corporation or a limited liability company. Under the Act a natural person receives substantial economic benefits from the assets of a corporation or a limited liability company if the person has more than a specified interest, as established by the Secretary of the Treasury, in the funds or assets of the corporation or the limited liability company.

The Act exempts many types of companies. The most significant exemptions are (1) a firm that employs more than twenty people and on its tax return reports revenues exceeding $5 million, (2) is a reporting company under the Securities Exchange act, or (3) a firm that is closely regulated, regulated by the Securities and Exchange Commission (e.g., broker-dealer) or the Office of the Comptroller of the Company (e.g., bank).

2. LLCS AND THE DISTINCT ENTITY CONCEPT

B. SUITS ON BEHALF OF THE LLC

Page 669.** Insert the following after *Tzolis v. Wolff*:

Section 802 of the Uniform Limited Liability Act and Section 18–1001 of the Delaware Limited Liability Act authorize derivative suits. A very different approach is taken in states that have patterned their statutes on the Prototype Act that was drafted in 1992 by the Subcommittee on

---

*   Insert at Page 472 in the Condensed Edition.

**   Insert at Page 481 before *Elf AtoChem North America* in the Condensed Edition.

Limited Liability Companies, Committee on Partnerships and Unincorporated Business Organizations of the Business Law Section of the American Bar Association. See 3 L. Ribstein & R. Keatinge, Limited Liability Companies (2d Ed. 2011) Appendix C, p. App C-109.

The Prototype Act does not authorize derivative suits; rather the act provides that an action in the name of the corporation can be initiated by a member or manager following impartial approval of the managers or members. The plaintiff's failure to obtain such approval cannot proceed on the basis the action being a derivative action. *See*, Saunders v. Briner, 334 Conn. 135, 160 n.26, 221 A.3d 1, 17 n. 26 (2019).

> The type of action contemplated in the Prototype Act differs from a derivative action, the drafters explained, because § 1102 of the Prototype Act creates procedures to permit disinterested members or managers who agree to sue in the company's name to bring an action—that is, to initiate a suit by the company—rather than permitting "a single member to sue on behalf of the [limited liability company] . . ." See 3 L. Ribstein & R. Keatinge, supra, p. App. C-109; id., pp. App. C-109 through App. C-110 ("[s]uit by a single member arguably is appropriate in public corporations because the members are generally passive and uninvolved in management and in any event too numerous to coordinate effectively for action against errant managers . . . [whereas] it may not be worth it in closely held firms like the typical [limited liability company] . . . [in which] members can be expected to be actively interested in the firm, and . . . can readily be coordinated for a vote on a suit by the firm"); J. Burkhard, "Resolving LLC Member Disputes in Connecticut, Massachusetts, Pennsylvania, Wisconsin, and the Other States that Enacted the Prototype LLC Act," 67 Bus. Law. 405, 409 (2012) (comparing derivative action's "dual purpose," in which shareholders first compel corporation to sue and then file suit on its behalf, with Prototype Act's direct action, which lacks precondition that company failed to act). . . . Burkhard and other commentators have noted that some courts, apparently overlooking commentary by the drafters of the Prototype Act, have conflated the member initiated action with the derivative action. See, e.g., J. Burkhard, supra, 67 Bus. Law. at 411 ("[i]n spite of the rather clear direction that Prototype Act [§] 1102 replaces the derivative suit . . . such has not always been how the courts have applied their respective statutes, and there appears to be substantial confusion among the courts as to how the statute should be applied"); A. Gladden, "Beyond Direct vs. Derivative: What *Muccio v. Hunt* Tells Us about Arkansas LLCs," 51 Ark. Law. 34, 35 (2016) (questioning decision of Arkansas Supreme Court applying shareholder derivative action principles to limited liability companies despite existence

of member initiated action in its limited liability company statute).

See also, Marx v. Morris, 286 Wis.2d 122, 148, 925 N.W.2d 112 (2019) (declining to recognize derivative suit in LLC where legislature has not expressly done so).

3. FIDUCIARY DUTIES

Page 671.* Insert the following case before *Salm v. Feldstein*:

Sky Harbor Hotel Props., LLC v. Patel Props., LLC (In re Sky Harbor Hotel Props., LLC)

Supreme Court of Arizona, 2019.
246 Ariz. 531, 443 P.3d 21.

■ CHIEF JUSTICE BALES, opinion of the Court:

These consolidated cases involve alleged breaches of fiduciary duties. To address these claims, the United States Bankruptcy Court for the District of Arizona certified the following questions to this Court:

1. Does a manager of an Arizona limited liability company ("LLC") owe common law fiduciary duties to the company?

2. Does a member of an Arizona LLC owe common law fiduciary duties to the company?

3. Can an Arizona LLC's operating agreement lawfully limit or eliminate those fiduciary duties?

We answer the first question in the affirmative. We answer the second question in the affirmative, provided that the member is an agent of the LLC. We answer the third question in the affirmative but note that the operating agreement may not eliminate the implied contractual duty of good faith and fair dealing.

I.

A.

Arizona enacted its first limited liability company act ("LLC Act") in 1992. . . .

The LLC Act does not expressly impose any fiduciary duties on members or managers. . . . By statute, however, "the law of agency" applies to the entire LLC Act. *See* A.R.S. § 29–854(B). We thus apply common law agency principles to answer the certified questions.

Arizona case law has not addressed these issues directly. . . .

"Absent controlling authority to the contrary, we generally follow the Restatement when it sets forth sound legal policy." *CSA 13-101 Loop, LLC v. Loop 101, LLC*, 236 Ariz. 410, 414 ¶ 18, 341 P.3d 452 (2014).

---

*   Page 483 in the Condensed Edition.

Under traditional agency rules, agency is the "fiduciary relation which results from the manifestation of consent by one person to another that the other shall act on his behalf and subject to his control, and consent by the other so to act." Restatement (Second) of Agency § 1 (Am. Law. Inst. 1958). The agent is the one who acts on behalf of another, the principal. *Id.* Agents are characterized by their "power to alter the legal relation between the principal and third persons and between the principal and" themselves. *Id.* § 12. Importantly, "[a]n agent is a fiduciary with respect to matters within the scope of his agency." *Id.* § 13.

We have characterized a fiduciary duty as imposing "the obligation of loyalty," *Ghiz v. Millett*, 71 Ariz. 4, 8, 222 P.2d 982 (1950), "the obligation of the utmost good faith in their dealings," *De Santis v. Dixon*, 72 Ariz. 345, 350, 236 P.2d 38 (1951), and "requiring a high degree of care," *Master Records, Inc. v. Backman*, 133 Ariz. 494, 497, 652 P.2d 1017 (1982) (quotations omitted). Thus, the nature of the fiduciary relationship for agents includes a duty of loyalty, a duty of good faith, and a duty of care. Partnerships, joint ventures, and corporations are all owed fiduciary duties by those empowered to act on behalf of such businesses. . . .

B.

By default, the members of an LLC are agents of the LLC "for the purpose of carrying on its business in the usual way." A.R.S. § 29–654(A)(1). However, if an LLC's management is vested in one or more managers, members are not automatically agents "solely by reason of being a member except to the extent that authority has been delegated to the member by" the manager or the operating agreement. § 29–654(B)(1). If management is vested in one or more managers, by law they are deemed agents of the LLC "for the purpose of carrying on its business in the usual way." § 29–654(B)(2). Thus, if an LLC is managed by one or more managers, such managers are agents, and under § 29–854 and agency law, they would owe common law fiduciary duties to the LLC.

The answer to the second question depends on whether management has been vested in one or more managers. If not, then all members are deemed agents of the LLC and thus would owe common law fiduciary duties to the LLC. If, however, the LLC is managed by one or more managers, members are considered its agents to the extent they have been delegated authority by the managers or the operating agreement under § 29–654(B)(1). Thus, a member owes common law fiduciary duties to the LLC if the member acts as an agent of the LLC.

C.

Although the common law recognizes that an LLC's managers or members, when acting as agents of the LLC, owe fiduciary duties to the company, these duties may be lawfully limited by a valid operating agreement.

The LLC Act provides for an operating agreement to govern relationships between members and managers and between managers, members, and the LLC itself. *See* A.R.S. § 29–682(B). The agreement "may contain any provision that is not contrary to law and that relates to . . . the rights, duties or powers of its members, managers, officers, employees or agents." *Id.* However, an LLC is not required to adopt an operating agreement. § 29–682(A) (stating that an LLC "may" adopt an agreement). Neither the LLC Act nor any other applicable law broadly prohibits an operating agreement from altering or limiting fiduciary duties that otherwise would be owed to the LLC by its managers or members.

The defendants in both certified cases concede that, regardless of their arguments relating to common law fiduciary duties, the implied covenant of good faith and fair dealing cannot be eliminated by an operating agreement. Based on public policy and case law, this is a well-supported concession. *See Rawlings v. Apodaca*, 151 Ariz. 149, 163, 726 P.2d 565 (1986) ("A covenant of good faith and fair dealing is implied in every contract . . . . The covenant . . . may be breached even though the express covenants of the contract are fully performed").

Thus, we answer the third question in the affirmative. Under the LLC Act, an operating agreement may lawfully limit or eliminate common law fiduciary duties owed to the LLC by its members or managers, although it may not erase the covenant of good faith and fair dealing implied in every contract. We have no occasion here to address whether the provisions of any particular operating agreement are contrary to law in this respect or otherwise.

II.

For the reasons noted, the LLC Act imposes common law fiduciary duties on managers and members serving as agents of the LLC. The LLC Act permits an LLC to limit or eliminate such common law duties through an operating agreement, except for the implied covenant of good faith and fair dealing.

4. DISASSOCIATION AND DISSOLUTION

Page 712.* Insert the following case before *Haley v. Talcott*.

Manere v. Collins

Appellate Court of Connecticut, 2020.
200 Conn. App. 356; 241 A.3d 133.

■ ELGO, J. . . .

In 2011, the plaintiff and Collins formed BAHR, a Connecticut limited liability company, for the purposes of purchasing and operating

---

*   Page 517 in the Concise Edition.

the [Seagrape] cafe. . . . The plaintiff and Collins were the sole members of BAHR, and the operating agreement designated both as its managers. Each provided capital contributions and "priority member loans" to BAHR. Specifically, Collins provided a $600 capital contribution and a $149,400 priority member loan, and the plaintiff provided a $400 capital contribution and a $19,600 priority member loan. Due to the disparity in their respective loans, Collins received a 60 percent interest and the plaintiff received a 40 percent interest in BAHR. Thereafter, the plaintiff signed a lease on behalf of BAHR for the property on which the cafe is located and further provided a personal guarantee of BAHR's performance under the lease.

In the fall of 2011, the cafe opened under BAHR's ownership. Because Collins was living in New York City, where he operated a different establishment, the plaintiff and Collins agreed that the plaintiff would be primarily responsible for operating the cafe and acting as its on-site manager. Prior to its opening, Collins and the plaintiff agreed that, as compensation for acting as the cafe's manager, the plaintiff would be paid a weekly salary of $600. The plaintiff's responsibilities included hiring and paying staff, obtaining stock items such as food and liquor, and accounting for revenue and expenses. Shortly after the cafe opened, the plaintiff and Collins agreed to raise the plaintiff's weekly salary to $1000 per week. Unbeknownst to Collins, the plaintiff was also using BAHR funds to pay for personal expenses such as health insurance, car payments, and gas. . . .

In 2015, Collins and his family moved to Connecticut and began to spend more time at the cafe. Due to his more active role in the cafe, Collins began to receive a weekly salary of $1000. . . . Later that same year, the plaintiff, Collins, and two associates of Collins opened a restaurant called the Georgetown Saloon. BAHR was not involved in this new venture. Instead, a separate limited liability company was formed for the purposes of owning and operating the Georgetown Saloon. Like his role at the cafe, the plaintiff was tasked with operating the Georgetown Saloon and acting as its on-site manager. Unlike the cafe, however, the Georgetown Saloon proved unsuccessful and closed in July, 2016. Although he did not blame the plaintiff for the Georgetown Saloon's failure, Collins became concerned with the plaintiff's style of management based on the manner in which the plaintiff conducted himself as its manager. As a result, Collins began to increasingly question the plaintiff about cafe affairs, including its finances and daily receipts.

Dissatisfied with the information he was receiving from the plaintiff, Collins began to ask cafe employees to text or e-mail him daily revenue numbers. When Collins asked the plaintiff to provide him with BAHR's business records—all of which had been relocated from the on-site office to the plaintiff's home after Hurricane Sandy—he received partial information which was often either incomplete or unresponsive. The piecemeal information provided by the plaintiff led Collins to perform his own inquiry into BAHR's records. . . . The trial court found Collins' reconstruction of the cafe's financial history revealed that the plaintiff had misappropriated approximately $190,000 of BAHR funds. In March, 2017, Collins unilaterally amended the operating agreement.[6] In the amended operating agreement, the plaintiff was terminated as a manager of BAHR. . . . The plaintiff's son, who was employed as a bartender at the cafe, was also terminated as an employee. Collins thereafter stopped payment on nine $1000 checks issued to the plaintiff and changed the locks on the cafe to prevent the plaintiff from accessing the building.

After taking over management of the cafe, Collins brought the building into compliance with fire safety standards. He further ensured that the cafe's staff were put on a payroll system for the purpose of placing the cafe in compliance with state and federal wage and hour laws. As a result, the cafe's revenue increased by 25 percent.

Since 2017, BAHR has not made any distributions to Collins or the plaintiff. Additionally, the plaintiff has not been provided with any information concerning BAHR's finances pursuant to the operating agreement, other than the information he received through the discovery process of the underlying litigation. Although Collins continued to receive a weekly salary of $1000 as of the time of the trial, no other payments have been made by BAHR to either Collins or the plaintiff.

In response to the measures taken by Collins, the plaintiff instituted the underlying action against Collins and BAHR, asserting a series of claims against both defendants including, inter alia, breach of contract by both defendants, breach of fiduciary duty by Collins, and oppression by Collins. The plaintiff also sought an accounting of BAHR's finances. The plaintiff further requested the dissolution of BAHR pursuant to § 34–267(a)(5) on the ground of oppression. In response, BAHR filed an answer and brought a counterclaim against the plaintiff. The plaintiff, as the counterclaim defendant, asserted four special defenses. After a two day bench trial, the court, *Hon. George R. Thim*, judge trial referee, rendered judgment in favor of the defendants on all counts of the plaintiff's complaint. The court further rendered judgment in favor of BAHR on its counterclaim and awarded it $190,463.03 in damages. This appeal followed. . . .

III

The plaintiff . . . claims that the court improperly rejected his application for a dissolution of BAHR pursuant to § 34–267(a)(5) on the ground of oppressive conduct by Collins. In response, the defendants assert that none of the actions taken by Collins amounted to oppression.

---

[6]   On appeal, the plaintiff does not challenge the court's finding that Collins is a 60 percent stakeholder in BAHR and, therefore, had authority to unilaterally amend the operating agreement.

We conclude that the court applied an incorrect legal standard in evaluating the plaintiff's claim under § 34–267(a)(5). We further conclude that a remand for a new trial on that claim is warranted in the present case. . . .

A

Section 34–267(a) provides that a limited liability company is to be dissolved, and its "activities and affairs must be wound up" in five different circumstances. Relevant to this claim, subdivision (5), provides the following: ". . . on the grounds that the managers or those members in control of the company: (A) Have acted, are acting or will act in a manner that is illegal or fraudulent; or (B) have acted or are acting in a manner that is oppressive and was, is, or will be directly harmful to the applicant . . . ." General Statutes § 34–267(a)(5). Neither this court nor our Supreme Court has had the opportunity to define oppression as that term has been utilized in § 34–267 since its inception. . . .

1 . . .

[W]e note that the Connecticut Uniform Limited Liability Company Act (CULLCA), General Statutes § 34–243 et seq., does not define "oppression." . . .

2

To begin our examination of extratextual sources, we believe it prudent to provide a review of the history of the oppression doctrine. . . . The history of the oppression doctrine reflects this specialized definition. As the modern corporate world began to take form during the nineteenth century, courts recognized that a pure majority rule for evaluating majority shareholder behavior "would lead to unfair results for minority shareholders" and, as a result, "used the trust metaphor to impose on directors a fiduciary duty to serve *all* of the shareholders of the corporation, not just a select group." (Emphasis in original.) D. Smith, "The Shareholder Primacy Norm," 23 J. Corp. L. 277, 310 (1998).

By the late nineteenth and early twentieth centuries, courts developed the oppression doctrine to reach conduct that the doctrines of ultra vires, fraud, and illegality did not address. . . . Indeed, courts remained reluctant to label majority shareholder conduct as fraudulent or to extend established legal doctrines to encompass such conduct, finding these "traditional grounds for imposing liability . . . too restrictive." Id., 314, 319. Consequentially, courts "continued to redress the concerns of minority shareholders, increasingly under the rubric of minority oppression." Id., 314. . . .

Both courts and scholars have underlined two competing standards that have been employed for analyzing whether conduct rises to the level of oppression: the "fair dealings" standard and the "reasonable expectations" standard. . . . see generally D. Moll, "Shareholder Oppression In Close Corporations: The Unanswered Question of

Perspective," 53 Vand. L. Rev. 749 (2000) (discussing competing standards used for oppression doctrine).

Under the "fair dealings" standard, oppression occurs when the conduct complained of is "burdensome, harsh and wrongful" and evinces either "a lack of probity and fair dealing in the affairs of a company to the prejudice of some of its members" or is "a visible departure from the standards of fair dealing, and a violation of fair play on which every shareholder who entrusts his money to a company is entitled to rely." (Internal quotation marks omitted.) *Ritchie v. Rupe*, supra, 443 S.W.3d 865. This test has been described as a focus "on preserving the majority's discretion to make decisions in furtherance of a legitimate business purpose—a standard that is typically satisfied when majority actions benefit the corporation." D. Moll, supra, 53 Vand. L. Rev. 762. Some courts employing the "fair dealings" standard have, however, cautioned that even though a majority shareholder's conduct was in furtherance of a legitimate business purpose, such conduct may be oppressive unless the minority shareholder "cannot demonstrate [that] a less harmful alternative" was available. *Daniels v. Thomas, Dean & Hoskins, Inc.*, 246 Mont. 125, 137–38, 804 P.2d 359 (1990).

In contrast, the "reasonable expectations" standard analyzes the conduct at issue from the perspective of the minority shareholder. As one Connecticut Superior Court decision aptly stated, oppression under this test "should be deemed to arise only when the majority conduct substantially defeats expectations that, objectively viewed, were both reasonable under the circumstances and were central to the petitioner's decision to join the venture." (Internal quotation marks omitted.) *Booth v. Waltz*, Superior Court, judicial district of Hartford, Docket No. CV-10-6011749-S, 2012 Conn. Super. LEXIS 3066 (December 14, 2012); see id. (defining oppression as that term appears in Connecticut Business Corporation Act, General Statutes § 33–600 et seq.). . . .

No court has had the occasion to directly address the issue of which test applies to claims of oppression pursuant to the RULLCA. We are convinced that, under the CULLCA, the "reasonable expectations" test is the proper standard to be applied for analyzing claims of oppression under § 34–267(a)(5). Our conclusion primarily rests on the commentary provided in § 701 of the RULLCA. . . . The commentary emphasizes that "[i]n many jurisdictions the concept [of oppression] equates to or at least includes the frustration of the plaintiff's reasonable expectations." Rev. Unif. Limited Liability Company Act of 2006 (2013) § 701, comment, 6C U.L.A. 135. In addition, the commentary provides guidance for assessing whether conduct is oppressive. . . . We see no cause or reason to suggest that the legislature intended for a different standard to apply under § 34–267(a)(5).

We further note that the majority of courts in other jurisdictions have embraced the "reasonable expectations" standard, or some iteration thereof, for claims of oppression in the close corporation context. . . .

The reasons that have been cited for this widespread acceptance of the "reasonable expectations" standard largely concern the unique nature of a closely held entity. See F. O'Neal & R. Thompson, Oppression of Minority Shareholders and LLC Members (Rev. 2d Ed. 2011), § 7:12, pp. 7–113 through 7–118. . . .

Like minority shareholders of a close corporation; . . . the unique features of an LLC therefore place a minority member in a special position, unlike his or her counterparts in a publicly traded company. As the Supreme Court of New Jersey explained in interpreting a statute with similar language, minority members of an LLC face a "unique vulnerability" for a number of reasons: "First, because the majority has a controlling interest, it has the power to dictate to the minority the manner in which the corporation is run. . . . Second, shareholders in close corporations frequently consist of family members or friends and once the personal relationship is destroyed, the company deteriorates. . . . Third, unlike shareholders in larger corporations, minority shareholders in a close corporation cannot readily sell their shares when they become dissatisfied with the management of the corporation. . . . Indeed, the discord in the corporation makes the minority stock even more difficult to sell." (Citations omitted; internal quotation marks omitted.) *Brenner v. Berkowitz*, supra, 134 N.J. 505. Thus, "[f]ocusing on the harm to the minority shareholder reflects a departure from the traditional focus, which was solely on the wrongdoing by those in control, and reflects the current trend of recognizing the special nature of close corporations." Id., 509.

Given that special nature and the unique position that a minority member holds, to focus on whether a majority member's conduct served a "legitimate business purpose" would, in our view, frustrate the protections that the oppression doctrine was intended to afford. . . . Thus, even when a majority member's conduct serves a legitimate business purpose that directly benefits the LLC, that conduct may be in direct contravention to a minority member's reasons for committing to the venture or the expectations that developed over time. Those reasons may have consisted of employment, a share of company earnings, or meaningful participation in its operations. See *Matter of Kemp & Beatley, Inc.*, supra, 64 N.Y.2d 72–73 . . . . The majority member's reasons for excluding a minority member from any of those expectations may benefit the LLC and could very well have not been achieved by less harmful means. In such circumstances, however, the minority member is left with "neither the power to dissolve the business unit at will, as does a partner in a partnership, nor does he have the 'way out' which is open to a shareholder in a publicly held corporation, the opportunity to sell his shares on the open market. . . . Thus, the illiquidity of a minority shareholder's interest in a close corporation renders him vulnerable to exploitation by the majority shareholders." *Meiselman v. Meiselman*, supra, 309 N.C. 291. In effect, the majority member is placed "in an enhanced power position to use the minority's investment without paying for it. . . . As a consequence, a [member] challenging the majority in a close corporation finds himself on the horns of a dilemma, he can neither profitably leave nor safely stay with the corporation. In reality, the only prospective buyer turns out to be the majority [member]." *Brenner v. Berkowitz*, supra, 134 N.J. 505. . . .

In light of the foregoing, we are persuaded that a proper analysis of an oppression claim requires the court to assess that claim under the "reasonable expectations" standard. Accordingly, we conclude that oppression, under the CULLCA, properly is analyzed under that standard. Thus, a majority member's conduct is oppressive if that conduct substantially defeats the minority member's expectations which, objectively viewed, were both reasonable under the circumstances and were central to his or her decision to join the venture or developed over time.

3

Having concluded that "oppression" under § 34–267(a)(5) should be assessed by the "reasonable expectations" standard, we believe it prudent to expand on the contours of that doctrine. As one court noted, "the key is *reasonable*." *Meiselman v. Meiselman*, supra, 309 N.C. 298. In our view, the RULLCA commentary sets forth a general list of factors that courts should consider when determining the reasonableness of a minority member's expectation. . . . [T]hese factors include "whether the expectation: (i) contradicts any term of the operating agreement or any reasonable implication of any term of that agreement; (ii) was central to the plaintiff's decision to become a member of the limited liability company or for a substantial time has been centrally important in the member's continuing membership; (iii) was known to other members, who expressly or impliedly acquiesced in it; (iv) is consistent with the reasonable expectations of all the members, including expectations pertaining to the plaintiff's [*390] conduct; and (v) is otherwise reasonable under the circumstances." Rev. Unif. Limited Liability Company Act of 2006 (2013) § 701, comment, 6C U.L.A., supra, p. 135.

There are a number of reasonable expectations that may drive a minority member to join an LLC by committing capital or expertise. "It is widely understood that, in addition to supplying capital to a contemplated or ongoing enterprise and expecting a fair and equal return, parties comprising the ownership of a close corporation may expect to be actively involved in its management and operation . . . ." *Matter of Kemp & Beatley, Inc.*, supra, 64 N.Y.2d 71. "In fact, because of the unique characteristics of close corporations, employment is often a vital component of a [close corporation] [member's] return on investment and a principal source of income." *Gunderson v. Alliance of Computer Professionals, Inc.*, supra, 628 N.W.2d 189 . . . .

Other reasonable expectations have included "possible entitlement to dividends, voting at shareholders' meetings, and access to corporate records." *Gimpel v. Bolstein*, supra, 125 Misc. 2d 53 . . . .

Notwithstanding these examples, the ULLCA factors also indicate—as do other courts—that the reasonableness of a member's expectation at the inception of an LLC may prove unreasonable over time and under particular circumstances. See *Meiselman v. Meiselman*, supra, 309 N.C. 298 (noting that reasonable expectations can be altered over time based on conduct of shareholders). For example, a minority member may reasonably expect to be employed by the LLC when entering into the venture with other members. That expectation, however, becomes patently unreasonable when, in light of the minority member's own misconduct, he or she is terminated from that employment with the LLC. "Accordingly, an expectation of continuing employment is not reasonable and oppression liability does not arise when the shareholder-employee's own misconduct or incompetence causes the termination of employment." *Gunderson v. Alliance of Computer Professionals, Inc.*, supra, 628 N.W.2d 192 . . . . This also extends to a member's expectation that a relative will be employed. See *Brenner v. Berkowitz*, supra, 134 N.J. 517–18 ("[W]hen the employment of the shareholder's relative is at issue, the shareholder will find it even more difficult to establish that those in control of a corporation acted oppressively. A heightened burden exists particularly in the case of a relative who was not employed at the beginning of the corporate relationship."). . . .

4

In addition to a finding of oppression, a court must determine, pursuant to § 34–267(a)(5)(B), whether the oppressive conduct "was, is, or will be directly harmful to the applicant . . . ." Notwithstanding this additional requirement, the CULLCA, its legislative history, and the ULLCA fail to define the harm that was, is, or will be suffered by the affected member. Generally, oppression consists of harm in the form of the defeat of a member's reasonable expectation. . . .

Because [e]very word and phrase [of a statute] is presumed to have meaning . . . we conclude that the language of § 34–267(a)(5)(B) requires a causal connection between the oppressive conduct and the harm sustained by the plaintiff-member. This requirement reflects the precept that, not only must a plaintiff establish that the conduct in question rose to the level of oppression, but he or she "must also demonstrate a nexus between that misconduct and the minority shareholder or her interest in the corporation. The remedies that a court will apply will logically depend on the harm to the minority shareholder or her interest in the corporation. . . . Therefore, in determining the nexus between the misconduct and the harm to the shareholder, the court must consider those acts that affect or jeopardize a shareholder's stock interest as well as those acts that may be specifically targeted to the shareholder." (Citation omitted.) *Brenner v. Berkowitz*, supra, 134 N.J. 508.

Moreover, the use of the disjunctive "or" in § 34–267(a)(5)(B) indicates that the legislature intended for a court to consider harm that is retrospective, active, or prospective. . . . Thus, under § 34–267(a)(5)(B), the harm at issue is not limited to a particular instance. So long as a member was harmed, is being harmed, or will be harmed by the oppressive conduct, such will suffice to satisfy the statute. We believe that allowing a court to form a remedy for oppressive behavior based on harm that has been or will be sustained by a plaintiff is in accord with the remedial nature that the statute was intended to provide. . . .

B

Turning to the facts of the present case, we conclude that the court applied an incorrect legal standard for assessing a claim alleging "oppression" pursuant to § 34–267(a)(5). . . .

In its memorandum of decision, the court made a number of factual findings to support its judgment in favor of Collins and BAHR with respect to the plaintiff's claim under § 34–267(a)(5). First, the court found that Collins had authority to amend the operating agreement based on its finding that, pursuant to the original operating agreement, he maintained a 60 percent interest in BAHR based on the outstanding priority loans still owed to him by BAHR. The court further found that Collins, as the majority member in BAHR, properly used his authority to remove the plaintiff as a manager of BAHR. Pursuant to § 11 of the amended operating agreement, Collins had complete control of BAHR because he was its sole manager. The court concluded that Collins' conduct in this respect "was not oppressive, harsh, or wrongful in light of [the plaintiff's] unfair dealing."

The court further found that Collins' failure to provide the plaintiff with financial documents, as required by the operating agreement, was not harmful to the plaintiff. In so finding, the court emphasized that the purpose of its requirement in the operating agreement was to enable BAHR's members to prepare their income tax statements. The court therefore concluded that the plaintiff was not harmed in this instance because all of BAHR's financial information was provided during the discovery process.

The court also rejected the plaintiff's oppression argument concerning Collins' termination of the plaintiff's son as an employee of the cafe and concerning the filing of a report with the Secretary of the State which omitted the plaintiff as a member of BAHR. The court reasoned that the plaintiff's son was terminated as an at-will employee because Collins believed that the plaintiff's son had provided incorrect information about the cafe's revenue. It further noted that the failure to file an accurate report with the Secretary of the State did "not appear to have been done with any intent to harm [the plaintiff]. This omission can be easily remedied. No harm has been shown."

Thus, the court concluded that the plaintiff failed to show that BAHR "should be dissolved under the provisions of [§ 34–267(a)(5)]. He has not shown [Collins'] conduct was illegal, oppressive, or in violation of [the plaintiff's] rights as a shareholder of BAHR. He has not shown that Collins has acted or is acting in a manner that is directly harmful to [the plaintiff]. Rather, the managerial actions taken by Collins were reasonable in light of [the plaintiff's] having used BAHR funds to pay personal expenses and his having withdrawn weekly 'salary' payments contrary to his agreement with Collins."

To begin, the court's memorandum of decision reflects that it did not employ the correct legal standard for determining whether the defendants' conduct was oppressive.[24] . . . "Ordinarily, the trial court's failure to apply the correct legal standard . . . results in a remand to the trial court for application of the correct standard."[25] . . .

It is clear from the record that the court did not assess the plaintiff's claim of oppression by focusing on his reasonable expectations as a minority member. Instead, the court improperly concentrated its analysis on Collins' conduct as a majority member in response to the plaintiff's misconduct as a manager of BAHR.

Notwithstanding the court's use of an incorrect legal standard, we believe that a new trial on the particular issue of the plaintiff's termination from employment is unwarranted. See *McDermott v. State*, supra, 316 Conn. 611. That is so because the reasonable expectations standard applied to the evidence adduced at trial would not change the court's factual findings or conclusion; specifically, the plaintiff's misappropriation of BAHR's funds would render any expectation of continuing employment by BAHR or the cafe unreasonable. . . . Upon our review of the record, the evidence strongly supports the court's conclusion that Collins' assumption of control over the management of the cafe "was not oppressive . . . in light of [the plaintiff's] unfair dealing." In addition, the record supports the court's conclusion that Collins had authority to do so pursuant to his majority stake in BAHR. The plaintiff may very well have reasonably expected to be employed by the cafe as its manager

---

[24]   In fact, during trial, the court expressly disallowed any testimony about the plaintiff's expectations upon forming BAHR with Collins and sustained an objection by the defendants on the basis that such testimony was irrelevant.

[25]   We further believe that the court's finding that the plaintiff failed to show that he was harmed does not appear to take into account the particular harms that arise from oppressive conduct *relative to the plaintiff's status as a minority member*. For instance, the court concluded that the plaintiff was not harmed by the defendants' failure to provide him with BAHR's financial documents because they were produced during the discovery process. This conclusion indicates that the court not only failed to consider the unique harms suffered by the plaintiff as a minority member, but it additionally ignored the fact that the plaintiff alleged these harms as a ground for oppressive conduct. See *Brenner v. Berkowitz*, supra, 134 N.J. 507. It was not until litigation proceedings began that the plaintiff received the company documents he believed he was entitled to. It would contravene the purposes of § 34–267(a)(5) if the only way that a minority member could exercise his or her rights would be to rely on the discovery process in the course of legal proceedings. Because the court did not appear to apply the correct legal standard for determining harm, we cannot affirm the court's judgment on that basis.

at the inception of BAHR, to remain as a manager of BAHR, and to have unobstructed access to both the cafe's premises and its bank accounts. Although those expectations may have, at one point, been reasonable, "it must be recognized that 'reasonable expectations' do not run only one way. To the extent that [the plaintiff] may have entertained 'reasonable expectations' of profit ... the other shareholders also entertained 'reasonable expectations' of fidelity and honesty from him. All such expectations were shattered when [the plaintiff] stole from the corporation. His own acts broke all bargains. . . . Since then, the only expectations he could reasonably entertain were those of a discovered thief: ostracism and prosecution." (Citation omitted.) *Gimpel v. Bolstein*, supra, 125 Misc. 2d 52.

To this end, we further note that, although it was the plaintiff's own misconduct which prompted the complained of acts he has alleged as oppressive, that misconduct does not obviate the need for the court to consider whether he continued to have reasonable expectations as a minority member. . . . While the plaintiff cannot establish oppression based on his termination of employment—or based on his being prevented from unfettered access to the cafe or BAHR's bank accounts— we emphasize that the plaintiff cannot be marginalized to the extent that he would be precluded from realizing what reasonable expectation he still maintains as a minority member.[26] . . .

Should the court find that the other acts taken by Collins were oppressive, the plaintiff's prior malfeasance should not bar his pursuit of an appropriate remedy under § 34–267(a)(5).[27] This is so because, so long

---

[26]   Given the atypical expectations of a minority member in an LLC, it is implausible that such a member would have committed capital to a venture in the knowledge that he or she could be entirely precluded from realizing any return on his or her investment. As one scholar on this issue has commented, a minority shareholder simply does not bargain for such a potentiality: "[I]t seems likely that minority shareholders would have refused to invest in the venture if the majority shareholder had insisted upon the retention of his freeze-out discretion. In other words, to appease the minority shareholders and to induce them to commit capital to the business, the majority shareholder would likely have had to promise that his freeze-out discretion would not be utilized." D. Moll, supra, 53 Vand. L. Rev. 799–800.

[27]   We emphasize that dissolution is not the sole remedy for oppression of a minority member. In fact, § 34–267(b) expressly permits a court to "order a remedy other than dissolution" for a proceeding brought under § 34–267(a)(5). In providing for these alternatives, this provision of the CULLCA suggests that the drafters acknowledged the extreme and drastic nature of dissolution as a remedy. . .

In *Bontempo v. Lare*, supra, 444 Md. 368–69, the Court of Appeals of Maryland adopted a nonexhaustive list of alternative remedies to dissolution for oppressive conduct that a court has at its disposal:

"(a)   The entry of an order requiring dissolution of the corporation at a specified future date, to become effective only in the event that the stockholders fail to resolve their differences prior to that date;

"(b)   The appointment of a receiver, not for the purposes of dissolution, but to continue the operation of the corporation for the benefit of all the stockholders, both majority and minority, until differences are resolved or 'oppressive' conduct ceases;

"(c)   The appointment of a 'special fiscal agent' to report to the court relating to the continued operation of the corporation, as a protection to its minority stockholders, and the retention of jurisdiction of the case by the court for that purpose;

as the plaintiff retains an investment in BAHR, his reasonable expectations include being entitled to certain minimum rights as a minority member. See *Gimpel v. Bolstein*, supra, 125 Misc. 2d 53 (although termination from employment for embezzling corporate funds was not oppression, minority shareholder was entitled to participate as "stranger" which includes "possible entitlement to dividends, voting at shareholders' meetings, and access to corporate records"). An infringement of these rights and a bar to any remedy leaves the plaintiff with a worthless asset. See *Brenner v. Berkowitz*, supra, 134 N.J. 505; *Meiselman v. Meiselman*, supra, 309 N.C. 291. We therefore conclude that a remand to the trial court for a new trial is warranted due to the court's failure to apply the correct legal standard as to the plaintiff's oppression claim under § 34–267(a)(5). . . .

* * *

On remand, *Manere v. Collins*, 2021 Conn. Super. LEXIS *10–11 (June 1, 2021), held:

> Although Collins and BAHR have acted in an oppressive manner and have harmed Manere, this court does not find that it should order a dissolution of BAHR at this time in view of all of the circumstances of this case. Instead, the court will instruct Collins and BAHR that they must act in a manner such that the reasonable expectations of Manere as a forty percent owner of BAHR are met by ensuring that Manere (i) timely receives information concerning the ongoing financial condition of

---

"(d)   The retention of jurisdiction of the case by the court for the protection of the minority stockholders without appointment of a receiver or 'special fiscal agent';

"(e)   The ordering of an accounting by the majority in control of the corporation for funds alleged to have been misappropriated;

"(f)   The issuance of an injunction to prohibit continuing acts of 'oppressive' conduct and which may include the reduction of salaries or bonus payments found to be unjustified or excessive;

"(g)   The ordering of affirmative relief by the required declaration of a dividend or a reduction and distribution of capital;

"(h)   The ordering of affirmative relief by the entry of an order requiring the corporation or a majority of its stockholders to purchase the stock of the minority stockholders at a price to be determined according to a specified formula or at a price determined by the court to be a fair and reasonable price;

"(i)   The ordering of affirmative relief by the entry of an order permitting minority stockholders to purchase additional stock under conditions specified by the court;

"(j)   An award of damages to minority stockholders as compensation for any injury suffered by them as the result of 'oppressive' conduct by the majority in control of the corporation."

See also *Brenner v. Berkowitz*, supra, 134 N.J. 514–15 (providing similar list of nonexclusive equitable remedies, short of dissolution, for oppressed minority shareholder).

We further note that, in fashioning a less drastic remedy, "a court should take into account not only the reasonable expectations of the oppressed minority [member], but also the expectations and interests of others associated with the company." *Bontempo v. Lare*, supra, 444 Md. 370. To do so necessarily requires a balancing of factors to make an equitable determination, and, therefore, is left to the sound discretion of the trial court. See *T & M Building Co. v. Hastings*, 194 Conn. App. 532, 551, 221 A.3d 857 (2019), cert. denied, 334 Conn. 926, 224 A.3d 162 (2020).

BAHR, (ii) receives notices of intended significant decisions by BAHR's members and Manager, including decisions concerning the potential distribution of profits, (iii) has the ability to reasonably inspect the records of the company, and to conduct reasonable audits thereof, and (iv) receives proportional and reasonable sharing in the profits of the company subject to any appropriate set off. Further, Collins and BAHR must also ensure that they act in a manner that is consistent with the terms of the operating agreement and applicable law.

The court will maintain jurisdiction so that the parties may petition the court to assess any ongoing issues. Further if issues remain ongoing, the court may reconsider whether BAHR should be dissolved.

CHAPTER 10

THE DUTY TO ACT WITH CARE, IN GOOD FAITH, AND LAWFULLY

1. THE DUTY OF CARE

C. THE DUTY TO MONITOR, COMPLIANCE PROGRAMS, AND INTERNAL CONTROLS

Page 775.* Add the next case before *In re Massey Energy Company*:

Marchand v. Barnhill

Supreme Court of Delaware, 2019.
212 A.3d 805.

■ **Judges:** Before STRINE, CHIEF JUSTICE; VALIHURA, VAUGHN, SEITZ, and TRAYNOR, JUSTICES, constituting the Court en Banc.

■ STRINE, CHIEF JUSTICE:

Blue Bell Creameries USA, Inc., one of the country's largest ice cream manufacturers, suffered a *listeria* outbreak in early 2015, causing the company to recall all of its products, shut down production at all of its plants, and lay off over a third of its workforce. Blue Bell's failure to contain *listeria*'s spread in its manufacturing plants caused *listeria* to be present in its products and had sad consequences. Three people died as a result of the *listeria* outbreak. Less consequentially, but nonetheless important for this litigation, stockholders also suffered losses because, after the operational shutdown, Blue Bell suffered a liquidity crisis that forced it to accept a dilutive private equity investment.

Based on these unfortunate events, a stockholder brought a derivative suit against two key executives and against Blue Bell's directors claiming breaches of the defendants' fiduciary duties. The complaint alleges that the . . . directors breached their duty of loyalty under *Caremark*. . .

As to the *Caremark* claim, the Court of Chancery held that the plaintiff did not plead any facts to support "his contention that the [Blue Bell] Board 'utterly' failed to adopt or implement any reporting and compliance systems." Although the plaintiff argued that Blue Bell's board had no supervisory structure in place to oversee "health, safety and sanitation controls and compliance," the Court of Chancery reasoned that

---

*   Page 577 in the Condensed Edition.

"[w]hat Plaintiff really attempts to challenge is not the existence of monitoring and reporting controls, but the effectiveness of monitoring and reporting controls in particular instances," and "[t]his is not a valid theory under . . . *Caremark*."

In this opinion, we reverse . . . .

I.   Background

A.   *Blue Bell's History and Operating Environment*

i.   *History*

Founded in 1907 in Brenham, Texas, Blue Bell Creameries USA, Inc. ("Blue Bell"), a Delaware corporation, produces and distributes ice cream under the Blue Bell banner. By 1919, Blue Bell's predecessor was struggling financially. Blue Bell's board turned to E.F. Kruse, who took over the company that year and turned it around. Under his leadership, the company expanded and became profitable.

E.F. Kruse led the company until his unexpected death in 1951. Upon his death, his sons, Ed F. Kruse and Howard Kruse, took over the company's management. Rapid expansion continued under Ed and Howard's leadership. In 2004, Ed Kruse's son, Paul Kruse, took over management, becoming Blue Bell's President and CEO. Ten years later, in 2014, Paul Kruse also assumed the position of Chairman of the Board, taking the position from his retiring father.

ii.   *The Regulated Nature of Blue Bell's Industry*

As a U.S. food manufacturer, Blue Bell operates in a heavily regulated industry. . . .

Specifically, FDA regulations require food manufacturers to conduct operations "with adequate sanitation principles" and, in line with that obligation, "must prepare . . . and implement a written food safety plan." As part of a manufacturer's food safety plan, the manufacturer must include processes for conducting a hazard analysis that identifies possible food safety hazards, identifies and implements preventative controls to limit potential food hazards, implements process controls, implements sanitation controls, and monitors these preventative controls. Appropriate corporate officials must monitor these preventative controls.

Not only is Blue Bell subject to federal regulations, but it must also adhere to various state regulations. At the time of the *listeria* outbreak, Blue Bell operated in three states, and each had issued rules and regulations regarding the proper handling and production of food to ensure food safety.

B.   *Plaintiff's Complaint* . . .

The complaint starts by observing that, as a single-product food company, food safety is of obvious importance to Blue Bell. But despite the critical nature of food safety for Blue Bell's continued success, the complaint alleges that management turned a blind eye to red and yellow flags that were waved in front of it by regulators and its own tests, and the board—by failing to implement any system to monitor the company's food safety compliance programs—was unaware of any problems until it was too late.

i.   The Run-Up to the Listeria Outbreak

According to the complaint, Blue Bell's issues began to emerge in 2009. . . .[From 2009 to 2013, both the FDA and state regulators found troubling compliance failures at Blue Bell's facilities. Moreover, in 2013, the Company received two reports from a third party laboratory that its Oklahoma facility tested positive for *Listeria*. Despite these reports, the complaint alleges managements did not share the information with the board and board minutes reflected no discussion at any of the intervening board meetings of *Listeria*. Matters did not improve in 2014; despite management being aware of 10 positive tests of *Listeria* in 2014, the complaint alleges that this information never made its way to the board. Quite the opposite was reported as the Vice-President of Operations reported to the board "the recent Silliker audit [Blue Bell's third-party auditor for sanitation issues in 2014] went well."] This lone reference to a third-party audit is the only instance, until the *listeria* outbreak forced the recall of Blue Bell's products, of *any* board-level discussion regarding food safety.

At this stage of the case, we are bound to draw all fair inferences in the plaintiff's favor from the well-pled facts. Based on this chronology of events, the plaintiffs have fairly pled that:

- Blue Bell had no board committee charged with monitoring food safety;

- Blue Bell's full board did not have a process where a portion of the board's meetings each year, for example either quarterly or biannually, were specifically devoted to food safety compliance; and

- The Blue Bell board did not have a protocol requiring or have any expectation that management would deliver key food safety compliance reports or summaries of these reports to the board on a consistent and mandatory basis. In fact, it is inferable that there was no expectation of reporting to the board of any kind.

In short, the complaint pleads that the Blue Bell board had made no effort at all to implement a board-level system of mandatory reporting of any kind.

[The facts are as follows. The board first discussed the *listeria* problem in late February 2015, four days after Blue Bell initiated a limited product recall. The recall occurred just a couple of days after the 2015 annual stockholders meeting even though on the cusp of that meeting state officials were raising concerns in the face of the expanding presence of *listeria* among Blue Bell's products. In March 2015 state health officials reported concerns of there being a connection between *listeria* infections and Blue Bell products.] The outbreak in Kansas matched a *listeria* strain found in Blue Bell's products in South Carolina. And by March 23, 2015, Blue Bell was forced to recall more products. Two days later, Blue Bell's board met and adopted a resolution "express[ing] support for Blue Bell's CEO, management, and employees and encourag[ing] them to ensure that everything Blue Bell manufacture[s] and distributes is a wholesome and good testing [sic] product that our consumers deserve and expect."

Blue Bell expanded the recall two weeks later, and less than a month later, on April 20, 2015, Blue Bell "instituted a recall of all products." By this point, the Center for Disease Controls and Prevention ("CDC") had begun an investigation and discovered that the source of the *listeria* outbreak in Kansas was caused by Blue Bell's Texas and Oklahoma plants. Ultimately, five adults in Kansas and three adults in Texas were sickened by Blue Bell's products; three of the five Kansas adults died because of complications due to *listeria* infection. The CDC issued a recall to grocers and retailers, alerting them to the contamination and warning them against selling the products.

After Blue Bell's full product recall, the FDA inspected each of the company's three plants. Each was found to have major deficiencies. . . . With its operations shuttered, Blue Bell faced a liquidity crisis. . . .

C.   *The Court of Chancery Dismisses the Case . . .*

The Court of Chancery . . . rejected the plaintiffs . . . claim that Blue Bell's directors breached their duty of loyalty under *Caremark* by failing to "institute a system of controls and reporting" regarding food safety. In support of this claim, the plaintiff asserted, based on the facts alleged in the complaint and reasonable inferences from those facts, that: (1) the Blue Bell board had no committee overseeing food safety; (2) Blue Bell's board did not have any reporting system in place about food safety; (3) management knew about the growing *listeria* issues but did not report those issues to the board, further evidence that the board had no food safety reporting system in place; and (4) the board did not discuss food safety at its regular board meetings.

. . . [T]he Vice Chancellor started by observing that "[d]espite the far-reaching regulatory schemes that governed Blue Bell's operations at the time of the [*l*]*isteria* contamination, the Complaint contains no allegations that Blue Bell failed to implement the monitoring and reporting systems required by the FDCA [Federal Food, Drug, and Cosmetic Act], FDA regulations or state statutes (or that it was ever cited for such a failure)." In fact, the Court of Chancery concluded that "documents incorporated by reference in the Complaint reveal that Blue Bell distributed a sanitation manual with standard operating and reporting procedures, and promulgated written procedures for processing and reporting consumer complaints." And at the board level, the Vice

Chancellor noted that "[b]oth Bridges and Paul Kruse ... provided regular reports regarding Blue Bell operations to the ... Board," including reports about audits of Blue Bell's facilities.

Based on Blue Bell's compliance with FDA regulations, ongoing third-party monitoring for contamination, and consistent reporting by senior management to Blue Bell's board on operations, the Court of Chancery concluded that there was a monitoring system in place. At bottom, the Court of Chancery opined that "[w]hat Plaintiff really attempts to challenge is not the *existence* of monitoring and reporting controls, but the *effectiveness* of monitoring and reporting controls in particular instances." That, the Court of Chancery held, does not state a *Caremark* claim. . . .

II. Analysis . . .

Although *Caremark* claims are difficult to plead and ultimately to prove out, we nonetheless disagree with the Court of Chancery's decision to dismiss the plaintiff's claim against the Blue Bell board.

Under *Caremark* and *Stone v. Ritter*, a director must make a good faith effort to oversee the company's operations. Failing to make that good faith effort breaches the duty of loyalty and can expose a director to liability. In other words, for a plaintiff to prevail on a *Caremark* claim, the plaintiff must show that a fiduciary acted in bad faith—"the state of mind traditionally used to define the mindset of a disloyal director."

Bad faith is established, under *Caremark*, when "the directors [completely] fail[ ] to implement any reporting or information system or controls[,] or ... having implemented such a system or controls, consciously fail[ ] to monitor or oversee its operations thus disabling themselves from being informed of risks or problems requiring their attention." In short, to satisfy their duty of loyalty, directors must make a good faith effort to implement an oversight system and then monitor it.

As with any other disinterested business judgment, directors have great discretion to design context-and industry-specific approaches tailored to their companies' businesses and resources.[103] But *Caremark* does have a bottom-line requirement that is important: the board must make a good faith effort—*i.e.*, try—to put in place a reasonable board-level system of monitoring and reporting.[104] Thus, our case law gives

---

[103]   *In re Citigroup Inc. S'holder Derivative Litig.*, 964 A.2d 106, 125–26 (Del. Ch. 2009) (Chandler, C.) (noting that *Caremark* "does not eviscerate the core protections of the business judgment rule"); *Caremark*, 698 A.2d at 970 ("Obviously the level of detail that is appropriate for such an information system is a question of business judgment."); *Desimone*, 924 A.2d at 935 n.95 (noting that the approaches boards take to monitoring the corporation under their *Caremark* duty "will obviously vary because of the different circumstances corporations confront"); *see also Caremark*, 698 A.2d at 971 ("But, of course, the duty to act in good faith to be informed cannot be thought to require directors to possess detailed information about all aspects of the operation of the enterprise. Such a requirement would simple [sic] be inconsistent with the scale and scope of efficient organization size in this technological age.").

[104]   *Stone*, 911 A.2d at 370; *see also Caremark*, 698 A.2d at 971 ("Generally where a claim of directorial liability for corporate loss is predicated upon ignorance of liability creating activities within the corporation, ... only a sustained or systematic failure of the board to

deference to boards and has dismissed *Caremark* cases even when illegal or harmful company activities escaped detection, when the plaintiffs have been unable to plead that the board failed to make the required good faith effort to put a reasonable compliance and reporting system in place.

For that reason, our focus here is on the key issue of whether the plaintiff has pled facts from which we can infer that Blue Bell's board made no effort to put in place a board-level compliance system. That is, we are not examining the effectiveness of a board-level compliance and reporting system after the fact. Rather, we are focusing on whether the complaint pleads facts supporting a reasonable inference that the board did not undertake good faith efforts to put a board-level system of monitoring and reporting in place.

Under *Caremark*, a director may be held liable if she acts in bad faith in the sense that she made no good faith effort to ensure that the company had in place any "system of controls."[106] Here, the plaintiff did as our law encourages and sought out books and records about the extent of board-level compliance efforts at Blue Bell regarding what has to be one of the most central issues at the company: whether it is ensuring that the only product it makes—ice cream—is safe to eat. Using these books and records, the complaint fairly alleges that before the *listeria* outbreak engulfed the company:

- no board committee that addressed food safety existed;

- no regular process or protocols that required management to keep the board apprised of food safety compliance practices, risks, or reports existed;

- no schedule for the board to consider on a regular basis, such as quarterly or biannually, any key food safety risks existed;

- during a key period leading up to the deaths of three customers, management received reports that contained what could be considered red, or at least yellow, flags, and the board minutes of the relevant period revealed no evidence that these were disclosed to the board;

- the board was given certain favorable information about food safety by management, but was not given important reports that presented a much different picture; and

exercise oversight—such as an utter failure to attempt to assure a reasonable information and reporting system exists—will establish the lack of good faith that is a necessary condition to liability.").

[106] *Stone*, 911 A.2d at 370; *see also Caremark*, 698 A.2d at 971 ("Generally where a claim of directorial liability for corporate loss is predicated upon ignorance of liability creating activities within the corporation, . . . only a sustained or systematic failure of the board to exercise oversight—such as an utter failure to attempt to assure a reasonable information and reporting system exists—will establish the lack of good faith that is a necessary condition to liability.").

- the board meetings are devoid of any suggestion that there was any regular discussion of food safety issues.

And the complaint goes on to allege that after the *listeria* outbreak, the FDA discovered a number of systematic deficiencies in all of Blue Bell's plants—such as plants being constructed "in such a manner as to [not] prevent drip and condensate from contaminating food, food-contact surfaces, and food-packing material"—that might have been rectified had any reasonable reporting system that required management to relay food safety information to the board on an ongoing basis been in place.

In sum, the complaint supports an inference that no system of board-level compliance monitoring and reporting existed at Blue Bell. Although *Caremark* is a tough standard for plaintiffs to meet, the plaintiff has met it here. When a plaintiff can plead an inference that a board has undertaken no efforts to make sure it is informed of a compliance issue intrinsically critical to the company's business operation, then that supports an inference that the board has not made the good faith effort that *Caremark* requires.

In defending this case, the directors largely point out that by law Blue Bell had to meet FDA and state regulatory requirements for food safety, and that the company had in place certain manuals for employees regarding safety practices and commissioned audits from time to time. In the same vein, the directors emphasize that the government regularly inspected Blue Bell's facilities, and Blue Bell management got the results.

But the fact that Blue Bell nominally complied with FDA regulations does not imply that the *board* implemented a system to monitor food safety *at the board level*. Indeed, these types of routine regulatory requirements, although important, are not typically directed at the board. At best, Blue Bell's compliance with these requirements shows only that management was following, in a nominal way, certain standard requirements of state and federal law. It does not rationally suggest that the board implemented a reporting system to monitor food safety or Blue Bell's operational performance. The mundane reality that Blue Bell is in a highly regulated industry and complied with some of the applicable regulations does not foreclose any pleading-stage inference that the directors' lack of attentiveness rose to the level of bad faith indifference required to state a *Caremark* claim.

In answering the plaintiff's argument, the Blue Bell directors also stress that management regularly reported to them on "operational issues." This response is telling. In decisions dismissing *Caremark* claims, the plaintiffs usually lose because they must concede the existence of board-level systems of monitoring and oversight such as a relevant committee, a regular protocol requiring board-level reports about the relevant risks, or the board's use of third-party monitors, auditors, or consultants. For example, in *Stone v. Ritter*, although the company paid $50 million in fines related "to the failure by bank employees" to comply with "the federal Bank Secrecy Act," the "[b]oard dedicated considerable resources to the [Bank Secrecy Act] compliance program and put into place numerous procedures and systems to attempt to ensure compliance." Accordingly, this Court affirmed the Court of Chancery's dismissal of a *Caremark* claim. Here, the Blue Bell directors just argue that because Blue Bell management, in its discretion, discussed general operations with the board, a *Caremark* claim is not stated.

But if that were the case, then *Caremark* would be a chimera. At every board meeting of any company, it is likely that management will touch on some operational issue. Although *Caremark* may not require as much as some commentators wish, it does require that a board make a good faith effort to put in place a reasonable system of monitoring and reporting about the corporation's central compliance risks. In Blue Bell's case, food safety was essential and mission critical. The complaint pled facts supporting a fair inference that no board-level system of monitoring or reporting on food safety existed.

If *Caremark* means anything, it is that a corporate board must make a good faith effort to exercise its duty of care. A failure to make that effort constitutes a breach of the duty of loyalty. . . .

III. Conclusion

We therefore reverse the Court of Chancery's decision and remand for proceedings consistent with this opinion.

Page 781. Insert the following after the first full paragraph:

The U.S. Department of Justice provides extensive guidance regarding the prosecutor's assessment of a firm's compliance program. The guidance is meant to assist prosecutors in making informed decisions whether and to what extent the company's compliance program was effective at the time of the offense as well at the time of the charging decision. Numerous matters are to be considered such as whether the program is appropriately designed (e.g., devotes appropriate attention and resources to high-risk transactions), establishes policies and procedures that incorporate a culture of compliance into day-to-day operations, includes periodic training of personnel, is regularly reevaluated and updated, and includes trustworthy mechanisms by which employees can anonymously or confidentially report possible wrongdoing. An important consideration is whether the company regularly reevaluates its program and adjusts it to changes in its regulatory or operating environment. *See* U.S. Department of Justice Criminal Division, Evaluation of Corporate Compliance Programs (April 2019).

In the face of both the Sentencing Guidelines and the Department of Justice directive to its prosecutors, according to an extensive study law compliance committees a rare among public companies:

> Our results show that companies are more likely to adopt compliance committees if they have been targets of prosecution and

if one of their board members has outside experience with using a CC. However, there is surprisingly little evidence that companies for which compliance investment is likely to be more valuable—in regulated industries or industries facing increased levels of prosecution activity—are likely to adopt CCs. More fundamentally, the overall level of adoption of compliance committees among public companies is still extremely low: less than 5%.

John Armour, Brandon Garrett, Jeffrey Gordon & Geeyoung Min, Board Compliance, 104 Minn. L. Rev. 1191, 1255 (2019). What can explain the absence of a board compliance committee?

Page 784.* Insert the following at the end of section C:

NOTE ON THE ROAD TO ENFORCING *CAREMARK* OBLIGATIONS

As will be seen in subsequent materials, there are two major obstacles private litigants must overcome to enforce *Caremark*. First, as discussed in the next section, "Liability Shields," the plaintiff must circumvent the immunity shield that most corporations now have in their articles of incorporation protecting directors (and now officers in Delaware) from liability for conduct that does not rise to the level of bad faith or self-dealing. Second, *Caremark* typically is pursued as a claim by the corporation that is brought by a shareholder who satisfies certain conditions—one such condition is the so-called demand requirement, discussed later, whereby the suit can proceed if the complaint pleads sufficient facts to indicate the board of directors had engaged in improper oversight. Many *Caremark* claims are dismissed because the suit's plaintiff is unable to persuade the court to excuse the demand requirement. For example, in *Firemen's Ret. Sys. of St. Louis v. Sorenson*, 2021 W.L. 4593777 (Del. Ch., Oct. 5, 2021), the complaint alleged that the board of directors was grossly inattentive of the vulnerability of Marriott's cybersecurity system. The court reasoned that allegations that the board's lax oversight caused the firm not to comply with non-binding cybersecurity standards was not enough to establish conscious and bad faith action by the directors so that the board was deemed sufficiently independent to consider whether the derivative suit should be pursued. As such, the demand on the board was not excused.

On the other hand, *Caremark*-based claims against Boeing Company's directors alleging the mishandling of safety warnings in connection with the Boeing 737 Max yielded a sizable settlement. The complaint alleged that as a result of the board's lack of oversight Boeing suffered nearly twenty billion dollars in losses including those for two airplane accidents that claimed 346 lives. A $237.5 million settlement by the company's D&O insurer was accompanied by certain governance changes including the creation of an independent ombudsman charged with interfacing with employee whistleblowers raising safety concerns.

---

*   Page 583 in the Concise Edition.

CHAPTER 11

THE DUTY OF LOYALTY

1. SELF-INTERESTED TRANSACTIONS

Page 821.* Insert the following decision before the Note:

Wall Sys. v. Pompa

Supreme Court of Connecticut, 2017.
324 Conn. 718, 154 A.3d 989.

■ **Judges:** ROGERS, C. J., and PALMER, EVELEIGH, MCDONALD, ESPINOSA and ROBINSON, JS. ROGERS, C. J. In this opinion the other justices concurred.

■ ROGERS, C. J.

The primary issue raised by this appeal and cross appeal is the range of monetary remedies available to an employer once it has proven that its employee breached his common-law duty of loyalty. The plaintiff, Wall Systems, Inc., appeals from the judgment of the trial court awarding it damages of $43,200, plus statutory interest and attorney's fees, after concluding that the defendant, William Pompa, had breached his duty of loyalty by working simultaneously for the plaintiff and for a competitor, and further, by accepting three kickbacks from a subcontractor in connection with his work for the plaintiff. . . .

On appeal, the plaintiff claims that the trial court, in fashioning a remedy for the defendant's breach of loyalty, improperly declined to order that the defendant forfeit all of the compensation he had received during the period in question, both from the plaintiff and from its competitor. The defendant responds that the court's ruling in this regard was a proper exercise of its discretion. . . . We conclude that the trial court's award of damages had sufficient evidentiary support and that the court's refusal to order additional monetary relief was an appropriate exercise of its discretion. . . .

The following facts, which either were found by the trial court or are not disputed, are relevant to the appeal. The plaintiff is a building contractor comprised of various divisions. The defendant began working for the plaintiff in or around 1995, when the company was under different management, and ultimately became the head of its exterior insulation finish systems division. As division head, the defendant's duties included finding the plaintiff jobs with general contractors, estimating and bidding jobs, hiring and negotiating with subcontractors, obtaining materials, overseeing work, ensuring proper billing, and arranging

---

* Page 621 at end of Section 1 in the Condensed Edition.

payment for subcontractors. The defendant was considered part of the plaintiff's management team. He was well compensated by the plaintiff, receiving a base salary plus annual bonuses. From 2005 to 2010, the defendant received a total of approximately $894,000 in compensation from the plaintiff.

Among the subcontractors working regularly for the plaintiff, who were hired and supervised by the defendant, were MK Stucco . . . and B-Jan Stucco, LLC (B-Jan). MK Stucco was owned by Michael Kowalczyk, and B-Jan was co-owned by Michael Bochenek and his father.

In 2005, Richard Valerio, who previously had worked for the plaintiff as an employee and a subcontractor, became the plaintiff's owner. In the years that followed, the defendant received less compensation than that to which he believed he was entitled, leading to a breakdown in the employer-employee relationship.

Because he was dissatisfied with his reduced income from the plaintiff, the defendant began to work for MK Stucco as an independent contractor, doing estimating work for jobs that MK Stucco then would bid on. From 2005 to 2010, the defendant received a total of approximately $89,782 in compensation from MK Stucco for this work. The defendant never informed Valerio that he was working for MK Stucco, nor did he ask permission to do so. Some of the jobs that the defendant estimated for MK Stucco were jobs on which the plaintiff also submitted bids.

In the spring of 2010, Valerio became suspicious, believing that the defendant was working against company interests. Around that time, Bochenek informed Valerio that the defendant was demanding kickbacks from the plaintiff's subcontractors, in essence, increasing the cost of their jobs by adding extra work to their contracts, then demanding that one half of the additional amount paid by the plaintiff be returned, in cash, to the defendant personally. The plaintiff terminated the defendant's employment in October, 2010, and filed this action against him at that time. At some point thereafter, Valerio learned that the defendant also had been working for MK Stucco.

In [its] complaint . . . the plaintiff alleged that the defendant had breached the duty of loyalty that he owed by virtue of his employment by, inter alia, charging kickbacks to subcontractors and performing work on his own behalf, rather than the plaintiff's, during the plaintiff's work day. He further claimed that the defendant's actions constituted conversion, statutory theft and fraud. The plaintiff claimed that the defendant's malfeasance had caused it damages of more than $500,000 and that, in light of the statutory theft allegations, it was entitled to treble damages.[5] [T]he plaintiff alleged unjust enrichment and requested that the trial court impose a constructive trust over both of the [Pompas'] assets, contending that those assets included moneys belonging to the

---

5   General Statutes § 52–564 provides: "Any person who steals any property of another, or knowingly receives and conceals stolen property, shall pay the owner treble his damages."

plaintiff that the defendant wrongfully had obtained. The defendant filed a cross complaint and counterclaims against the plaintiff and Valerio alleging, in essence, that the plaintiff had not paid him all of the compensation to which he was entitled.

After a bench trial, the trial court held that the defendant had violated his duty of loyalty to the plaintiff by working for MK Stucco, a competitor of the plaintiff, and by receiving compensation for that work. It found that, although the plaintiff had performed only estimating duties for MK Stucco, and not bidding work, some of the jobs at issue had been bid on by both MK Stucco and the plaintiff. . . . In the court's view, the defendant's actions in this regard were deliberate, wrongful and intentional. The court further concluded, however, that the plaintiff had failed to prove that it had suffered any financial harm as a result of those actions. Specifically, there was no evidence that the plaintiff had lost any bids to MK Stucco due to the defendant's work for both companies, or that the defendant had worked for MK Stucco during the plaintiff's work day rather than on evenings or weekends, as he had testified without contradiction. Moreover, the plaintiff had not produced any evidence to show how much it would have earned on the jobs it purportedly had lost wrongfully, even assuming that the lost jobs were attributable to the defendant's actions or inactions.

The trial court held additionally that the defendant had breached his duty of loyalty to the plaintiff by engaging in a kickback scheme with B-Jan, but not with any other subcontractors. It relied particularly on testimony from Bochenek as to three jobs on which B-Jan was working as a subcontractor and, according to Bochenek, the defendant had effected an increase to the contract price and, thereafter, required B-Jan to return one half of the price increase, in cash, to the defendant personally. Because the amount of the contract increases for those jobs were, respectively, $7000, $1400 and $6000, the court concluded that the total proven damages to the plaintiff, as a result of the kickback scheme, were $14,400, i.e., the aggregate of the individual increases. The court further concluded that the defendant's actions vis-a-vis B-Jan constituted conversion, statutory theft, fraud and unjust enrichment and, on the basis of the statutory theft, tripled the damages found to result in an award to the plaintiff in the amount of $43,200. . . . As to the defendant's counterclaim for unpaid bonuses, the trial court rejected it as unsupported by the evidence.

Regarding the plaintiff's contention, advanced in its trial brief, that the defendant should be required to forfeit all of the compensation he had earned from both the plaintiff and from MK Stucco during the period of his disloyalty, the trial court . . . stated only that it was "not persuaded." In response to the plaintiff's motions for articulation/clarification and reconsideration, the court, after hearing argument, reiterated that there was no evidence that the plaintiff had been harmed due to the defendant's working for MK Stucco, and it observed that the plaintiff also had failed to prove its allegations as to the defendant requiring kickbacks from any subcontractor other than B-Jan. The court cited the amount of damages it had found flowing from the B-Jan kickbacks and noted that, even trebled, that amount was insignificant in comparison to the amount of compensation that the plaintiff believed the defendant should have to forfeit. The court elaborated that the plaintiff had worked for MK Stucco on his own time, and there was no evidence that that work had interfered with his work for the plaintiff. In making its ruling, the court expressly stated that it "has the discretion as to what damages go to the plaintiff . . . ." After an additional hearing was held for the determination of attorney's fees,[8] a final judgment was rendered. This appeal and cross appeal followed. Both the plaintiff and the defendant challenge the propriety of the trial court's monetary remedy, while Jill Pompa contends that the imposition of a constructive trust was unwarranted. We will address these claims in turn.

The plaintiff claims that the trial court, as a matter of law, improperly declined to order the defendant to forfeit everything he had earned between 2005 and 2010, because certain authority provides that a disloyal employee is not entitled to the compensation he was paid during a period of disloyalty. According to the plaintiff, when an employee, such as the defendant here, is radically unfaithful, or wilfully breaches his duty of loyalty, his employer is entitled to recover the employee's entire salary, and that such is the case even when there is no proof of specific damages to the employer. In the plaintiff's view, given the facts found, and the trial court's legal conclusions that the defendant committed fraud, conversion and statutory theft, the court was required to order the remedy of forfeiture. The plaintiff claims additionally that the defendant, due to his breach of loyalty, also should be required to disgorge the compensation that he had received from MK Stucco, regardless of whether he had worked for MK Stucco on his own, or the plaintiff's, time. . . .

The defendant responds that the amount of damages to be awarded for an employee's breach of his duty of loyalty is a matter within a trial court's discretion. He further contends that, given all of the circumstances, the trial court in the present case properly exercised its discretion in declining to order him to forfeit all of the compensation that he had earned from the plaintiff, and to disgorge that which he had received from MK Stucco, during his period of disloyalty. In the defendant's view, such a remedy would have been inequitable and harsh, particularly in light of the plaintiff's failure to prove that it had suffered any harm as a result of his working for MK Stucco. In response, the plaintiff points out that the court did find that it had suffered a financial loss in connection with the kickback scheme and that, in any event, proof

---

8   The trial court subsequently awarded the plaintiff attorney's fees of $24,609.75 and prejudgment interest of $19,833.96. . . .

of such a loss is unnecessary particularly because the defendant's breach was wilful and intentional.

We agree with the plaintiff that the remedies of forfeiture of compensation paid by an employer, and disgorgement of amounts received from third parties, are available when an employer proves that its employee has breached his or her duty of loyalty, regardless of whether the employer has proven damages as a result of that breach. Nevertheless, the remedies are not mandatory upon the finding of a breach of the duty of loyalty, intentional or otherwise, but rather, are discretionary ones whose imposition is dependent upon the equities of the case at hand. Moreover, while certain factors, including harm to the employer, should not preclude a finding that the employee has committed a breach of the duty of loyalty, they nevertheless may be considered in the fashioning of a remedy. Here, because the trial court properly exercised its broad discretion when it awarded damages but declined to order forfeiture or disgorgement, we will not disturb its judgment on this basis. . . .

"The relationship of principal and agent implies trust or confidence by the principal in the agent, and the agent is obligated to exercise the utmost good faith, loyalty and honesty toward his principal or employer. . . . The general principle for the agent's duty of loyalty according to the Restatement is that the agent must act solely for the benefit of the principal in matters connected with the agency." (Citation omitted.) *News America Marketing In-Store, Inc. v. Marquis*, 86 Conn. App. 527, 535, 862 A.2d 837 (2004), aff'd, 276 Conn. 310, 885 A.2d 758 (2005); see also 2 Restatement (Third), Agency § 8.01, comment (b), p. 250 (2006) ("the general fiduciary principle requires that the agent subordinate the agent's interests to those of the principal and place the principal's interests first as to matters connected with the agency relationship"). . . .

The duty of loyalty . . . includes the duty to refrain from acquiring material benefits from third parties in connection with transactions undertaken on the employer's behalf. 2 Restatement (Third), supra, § 8.02, p. 280. This rule bars the collection of secret commissions and kickbacks, "which might cause the employee to act at the expense or detriment of his or her employer." *In re Tri-Star Technologies Co.*, 257 B.R. 629, 635–36 (Bankr. D. Mass. 2001).

If an employer can prove an employee's breach of his or her duty of loyalty, there are a variety of remedies potentially available. An employer, like the plaintiff here, may invoke the court's equitable authority when seeking monetary relief, particularly when it has difficulty proving damages. "The law of restitution and unjust enrichment . . . creates a basis for an [employee's] liability to [an employer] when the [employee] breaches a fiduciary duty," even when no loss to the employer is shown. 2 Restatement (Third), supra, § 8.01 comment (d) (1), p. 258. More specifically, if an employee realizes a material benefit from a third party in connection with his breach of the duty of loyalty, the employee "is subject to liability to deliver the benefit, its proceeds, or its value to the [employer]." Id.; see also id., § 8.02, comment (e), p. 285. Accordingly, "[a]n employee who breaches the fiduciary duty of loyalty may be required to disgorge any profit or benefit he received as a result of his disloyal activities," regardless of whether the employer has suffered a corresponding loss. . . .

Additionally, "an employer may seek forfeiture of its employee's compensation." *Cameco, Inc. v. Gedicke*, 157 N.J. 504, 519, 724 A.2d 783 (1999). . . . Notably, however, even in cases in which a court orders forfeiture of compensation, the forfeiture normally is apportioned, that is, it is limited to the period of time during which the employee engaged in disloyal activity.

. . . Restatement (Second) of Agency discusses these remedies, along with the others previously summarized . . . in the commentary sections accompanying the rules that outline the duties of agents. . . . As to forfeiture, the commentary acknowledges and the case notes further indicate that, although it is a well recognized remedy, courts do not apply it in uniform fashion. . . .

[F]orfeiture and disgorgement are not legal remedies, but rather, are equitable ones. Generally speaking, "equitable determinations that depend on the balancing of many factors are committed to the sound discretion of the trial court." (Internal quotation marks omitted.) *Wendell Corp. Trustee v. Thurston*, 239 Conn. 109, 114, 680 A.2d 1314 (1996); see also *Connecticut Bank & Trust Co. v. Winters*, 225 Conn. 146, 162, 622 A.2d 536 (1993). . . . "[E]quitable discretion is not governed by fixed principles and definite rules . . . ." (Internal quotation marks omitted.) Id. Rather, implicit therein "is conscientious judgment directed by law and reason and looking to a just result." (Internal quotation marks omitted.) Id.

Equitable discretion is especially appropriate in cases involving breaches of the duty of loyalty due to their highly fact specific nature. *Id.*, 230–31. "The contexts giving rise to claims of employee disloyalty are so varied that they preclude the mechanical application of abstract rules of law." *Cameco, Inc. v. Gedicke*, supra, 157 N.J. 516. "[T]o require an agent to forfeit all compensation for every breach of fiduciary duty, or even every serious breach, would deprive the remedy of its equitable nature and would disserve its purpose of protecting relationships of trust." *Burrow v. Arce*, supra, 997 S.W.2d 241. In short, "the remedy of forfeiture must fit the circumstances presented." Id.; see also *American Timber & Trading Co. v. Niedermeyer*, 276 Or. 1135, 1155, 558 P.2d 1211 (1976) ("[t]he remedy of restoration of compensation is an equitable principle and its applicability is dependent upon the individual facts of each case").

For the foregoing reasons, we conclude that discretionary application of the remedies of forfeiture and disgorgement is both proper and desirable. In determining whether to invoke these remedies, a trial court

should consider all of the facts and circumstances of the case before it
.... The following [nonexclusive] ... factors [are]: the employee's
position, duties and degree of responsibility with the employer; the level
of compensation that the employee receives from the employer; the
frequency, timing and egregiousness of the employee's disloyal acts; the
wilfulness of the disloyal acts; the extent or degree of the employer's
knowledge of the employee's disloyal acts; the effect of the disloyal acts
on the value of the employee's properly performed services to the
employer; the potential for harm, or actual harm, to the employer's
business as a result of the disloyal acts; the degree of planning taken by
the employee to undermine the employer; and the adequacy of other
available remedies, as herein discussed. ... Additionally, when imposing
the remedy of forfeiture of compensation, depending on the
circumstances, a trial court may in its discretion apply apportionment
principles, rather than ordering a wholesale forfeiture that may be
disproportionate to the misconduct at issue. ... Conversely, the court
may conclude that all compensation should be forfeited because the
"employee's unusually egregious or reprehensible conduct pervaded and
corrupted the entire [employment] relationship." *Futch v. McAllister
Towing of Georgetown, Inc.*, supra, 610. ...

Regarding the trial court's discretionary ruling, the plaintiff did not
request apportionment.[13] Rather, it argued to the court that it was
entitled to recover all of the compensation that the defendant had
received from the plaintiff between 2005 and 2010, plus all of his pay
from MK Stucco, which together totaled approximately $1 million. In
declining to award those amounts to the plaintiff, the trial court
considered some of the factors that we have enumerated herein.
Specifically, in its written opinion, the court observed that the
defendant's disloyal acts were deliberate and intentional, and it
concluded that those acts constituted various other torts. Additionally,
the court made findings as to the defendant's managerial responsibilities,
his substantial compensation from the plaintiff and the specifics of his
disloyal acts. Nevertheless, in regard to the defendant's side work for MK
Stucco, the court found that the plaintiff had failed to prove that its
business had been harmed as a result of the defendant's actions, either
because it had lost bids that it otherwise would have been awarded or
because the defendant had performed duties for MK Stucco during the
plaintiff's workdays.[14] In regard to the kickback scheme, the court
reasoned that the plaintiff had failed to prove that much of what it had

---

[13]   Valerio testified that the plaintiff was paid $1600 per week. In other words, his
compensation was apportioned to specific periods of time. Furthermore, there was no evidence
that the defendant's disloyalty permeated every week in 2005 through 2010; rather, it appears
that it was sporadic.

[14]   The evidence showed that, between 2005 and 2010, the defendant had estimated only
thirty-five jobs for MK Stucco. See footnote 4 of this opinion. In contrast, the defendant testified
that he had worked on approximately 250 jobs per year for the plaintiff, while Valerio estimated
that it was between 100 and 200. The total compensation received by the defendant from MK
Stucco during this period was a small fraction of that which he received from the plaintiff.

alleged had even occurred, and the court concluded that the plaintiff's proven damages were negligible when compared to the large amount the plaintiff was seeking to recover. In the end, the court believed that the plaintiff's other remedies, which had led to a total award of $87,643.71, were adequate. See footnote 8 of this opinion. Notably, the court also denied the defendant's claims for unpaid wages.

In sum, the trial court weighed the specific facts and circumstances of the case to arrive at a fair and reasonable solution that, in the court's view, was not inequitable to either party. Accordingly, it properly exercised its equitable discretion to deny the relief requested. See *Rockefeller v. Grabow*, supra, 136 Idaho 643 ("[t]here is no abuse of discretion where the trial court perceives the issue in question as discretionary, acts within the outer limits of its discretion and consistently with the legal standards available . . . and reaches its own decision through an exercise of reason").

CHAPTER 12

THE ANTIFRAUD PROVISION: SECTION 10(b) AND RULE 10b–5

5. PRIMARY PARTICIPANTS AFTER *CENTRAL BANK*

Page 1017. Substitute the following for the lower court decision in *Lorenzo v. SEC*:

Lorenzo v. SEC
Supreme Court of the United States, 2019.
___ U.S. ___, 139 S. Ct. 1094.

■ JUSTICE BREYER delivered the opinion of the Court. . . .

In *Janus Capital Group, Inc. v. First Derivative Traders*, 564 U. S. 135 . . . (2011), we examined . . . Rule 10b–5(b), which forbids the "mak[ing]" of "any untrue statement of a material fact." We held that the "*maker* of a statement is the person or entity with ultimate authority over the statement, including its content and whether and how to communicate it." *Id.*, at 142 . . . (emphasis added). We said that "[w]ithout control, a person or entity can merely suggest what to say, not 'make' a statement in its own right." *Ibid.* And we illustrated our holding with an analogy: "[W]hen a speechwriter drafts a speech, the content is entirely within the control of the person who delivers it. And it is the speaker who takes credit—or blame—for what is ultimately said." *Id.*, at 143 . . . . On the facts of *Janus*, this meant that an investment adviser who had merely "participat[ed] in the drafting of a false statement" "made" by another could not be held liable in a private action under subsection (b) of Rule 10b–5. *Id.*, at 145 . . . .

In this case, we consider whether those who do not "make" statements (as *Janus* defined "make"), but who disseminate false or misleading statements to potential investors with the intent to defraud, can be found to have violated the *other* parts of Rule 10b–5, subsections (a) and (c) . . . We believe that they can.

I

A . . .

Francis Lorenzo, the petitioner, was the director of investment banking at Charles Vista, LLC, a registered broker-dealer in Staten Island, New York. Lorenzo's only investment banking client at the time was Waste2Energy Holdings, Inc., a company developing technology to convert "solid waste" into "clean renewable energy."

In a June 2009 public filing, Waste2Energy stated that its total assets were worth about $14 million. This figure included intangible assets, namely, intellectual property, valued at more than $10 million. Lorenzo was skeptical of this valuation, later testifying that the intangibles were a "dead asset" because the technology "didn't really work."

During the summer and early fall of 2009, Waste2Energy hired Lorenzo's firm, Charles Vista, to sell to investors $15 million worth of debentures, a form of "debt secured only by the debtor's earning power, not by a lien on any specific asset," Black's Law Dictionary 486 (10th ed. 2014).

In early October 2009, Waste2Energy publicly disclosed, and Lorenzo was told, that its intellectual property was worthless, that it had " ' "[w]rit[ten] off . . . all [of its] intangible assets," ' " and that its total assets (as of March 31, 2009) amounted to $370,552.

Shortly thereafter, on October 14, 2009, Lorenzo sent two e-mails to prospective investors describing the debenture offering. According to later testimony by Lorenzo, he sent the e-mails at the direction of his boss, who supplied the content and "approved" the messages. The e-mails described the investment in Waste2Energy as having "3 layers of protection," including $10 million in "confirmed assets." The e-mails nowhere revealed the fact that Waste2Energy had publicly stated that its assets were in fact worth less than $400,000. Lorenzo signed the e-mails with his own name, he identified himself as "Vice President—Investment Banking," and he invited the recipients to "call with any questions."

B

In 2013, the Securities and Exchange Commission instituted proceedings against Lorenzo (along with his boss and Charles Vista). The Commission charged that Lorenzo had violated Rule 10b–5, § 10(b) of the Exchange Act . . . . Ultimately, the Commission found that Lorenzo had run afoul of these provisions by sending false and misleading statements to investors with intent to defraud. As a sanction, it fined Lorenzo $15,000, ordered him to cease and desist from violating the securities laws, and barred him from working in the securities industry for life.

Lorenzo appealed [to the Court of Appeals for the District of Columbia], arguing primarily that in sending the e-mails he lacked the intent required to establish a violation of Rule 10b–5, § 10(b), and § 17(a)(1), which we have characterized as " 'a mental state embracing intent to deceive, manipulate, or defraud.' " *Aaron v. SEC*, 446 U. S. 680 . . . . With one judge dissenting, the Court of Appeals panel rejected Lorenzo's lack-of-intent argument. 872 F. 3d 578, 583 (CADC 2017). Lorenzo does not challenge the panel's scienter finding. . . .

Lorenzo also argued that, in light of *Janus*, he could not be held liable under subsection (b) of Rule 10b–5. 872 F. 3d, at 586–587. The panel agreed. Because his boss "asked Lorenzo to send the emails, supplied the central content, and approved the messages for distribution," *id.*, at 588, it was the boss that had "ultimate authority" over the content of the statement "and whether and how to communicate it," *Janus*, 563 U. S., at 142, 131 S. Ct. 2296, 180 L. Ed. 2d 166. (We took this case on the assumption that Lorenzo was not a "maker" under subsection (b) of Rule 10b–5, and do not revisit the court's decision on this point.)

The Court of Appeals nonetheless sustained (with one judge dissenting) the Commission's finding that, by knowingly disseminating false information to prospective investors, Lorenzo had violated other parts of Rule 10b–5, subsections (a) and (c), as well as § 10(b) . . . .

Lorenzo then filed a petition for certiorari in this Court. We granted review to resolve disagreement about whether someone who is not a "maker" of a misstatement under *Janus* can nevertheless be found to have violated the other subsections of Rule 10b–5 and related provisions of the securities laws, when the only conduct involved concerns a misstatement. . . .

II

A

At the outset, we review the relevant provisions of Rule 10b–5 and of the statutes. See Appendix, *infra*. As we have said, subsection (a) of the Rule makes it unlawful to "employ any device, scheme, or artifice to defraud." Subsection (b) makes it unlawful to "make any untrue statement of a material fact." And subsection (c) makes it unlawful to "engage in any act, practice, or course of business" that "operates . . . as a fraud or deceit." See 17 CFR § 240.10b–5. . . .

B . . .

It would seem obvious that the words in these provisions are, as ordinarily used, sufficiently broad to include within their scope the dissemination of false or misleading information with the intent to defraud. By sending emails he understood to contain material untruths, Lorenzo "employ[ed]" a "device," "scheme," and "artifice to defraud" within the meaning of subsection (a) of the Rule, § 10(b) . . . . By the same conduct, he "engage[d] in a[n] act, practice, or course of business" that "operate[d] . . . as a fraud or deceit" under subsection (c) of the Rule. Recall that Lorenzo does not challenge the appeals court's scienter finding, so we take for granted that he sent the emails with "intent to deceive, manipulate, or defraud" the recipients. *Aaron*, 446 U. S., at 686, n. 5 . . . . Under the circumstances, it is difficult to see how his actions could escape the reach of those provisions. . . .

These provisions capture a wide range of conduct. Applying them may present difficult problems of scope in borderline cases. Purpose, precedent, and circumstance could lead to narrowing their reach in other contexts. But we see nothing borderline about this case, where the relevant conduct (as found by the Commission) consists of disseminating false or misleading information to prospective investors with the intent to defraud. And while one can readily imagine other actors tangentially involved in dissemination—say, a mailroom clerk—for whom liability would typically be inappropriate, the petitioner in this case sent false statements directly to investors, invited them to follow up with questions, and did so in his capacity as vice president of an investment banking company.

C

Lorenzo argues that, despite the natural meaning of these provisions, they should not reach his conduct. This is so, he says, because the only way to be liable for false statements is through those provisions that refer *specifically* to false statements. Other provisions, he says, concern "scheme liability claims" and are violated only when conduct other than misstatements is involved. . . .

The premise of this argument is that each of these provisions should be read as governing different, mutually exclusive, spheres of conduct. But this Court and the Commission have long recognized considerable overlap among the subsections of the Rule and related provisions of the securities laws. See *Herman & MacLean v. Huddleston*, 459 U. S. 375, 383, 103 S. Ct. 683, 74 L. Ed. 2d 548 (1983) ("[I]t is hardly a novel proposition that" different portions of the securities laws "prohibit some of the same conduct" (internal quotation marks omitted)). . . . It is "understandable, therefore," that "in declaring certain practices unlawful," it was thought prudent "to include both a general proscription against fraudulent and deceptive practices and, out of an abundance of caution, a specific proscription against nondisclosure" even though "a specific proscription against nondisclosure" might in other circumstances be deemed "surplusage." *Id.*, at 198–199 . . . .

Coupled with the Rule's expansive language, which readily embraces the conduct before us, this considerable overlap suggests we should not hesitate to hold that Lorenzo's conduct ran afoul of subsections (a) and (c), as well as the related statutory provisions. Our conviction is strengthened by the fact that we here confront behavior that, though plainly fraudulent, might otherwise fall outside the scope of the Rule. Lorenzo's view that subsection (b), the making-false-statements provision, *exclusively* regulates conduct involving false or misleading statements would mean those who disseminate false statements with the intent to cheat investors might escape liability under the Rule altogether. But using false representations to induce the purchase of securities would seem a paradigmatic example of securities fraud. We do not know why Congress or the Commission would have wanted to disarm enforcement in this way. And we cannot easily reconcile Lorenzo's approach with the basic purpose behind these laws: "to substitute a philosophy of full disclosure for the philosophy of *caveat emptor* and thus to achieve a high standard of business ethics in the securities industry." *Capital Gains*, 375 U. S., at 186 . . . .

III

Lorenzo and the dissent make a few other important arguments. They contend that applying subsections (a) or (c) of Rule 10b–5 to conduct like his would render our decision in *Janus* . . .) "a dead letter". But we do not see how that is so. In *Janus*, we considered the language in subsection (b), which prohibits the "mak[ing]" of "any untrue statement of a material fact." See 564 U. S., at 141–143 . . . We held that the "maker" of a "statement" is the "person or entity with ultimate authority over the statement." *Id.*, at 142 . . . . And we found that subsection (b) did not (under the circumstances) cover an investment adviser who helped *draft* misstatements issued by a *different* entity that controlled the statements' content. *Id.*, at 146–148 . . . . We said nothing about the Rule's application to the dissemination of false or misleading information. And we can assume that *Janus* would remain relevant (and preclude liability) where an individual neither *makes* nor *disseminates* false information— provided, of course, that the individual is not involved in some other form of fraud.

Next, Lorenzo points to the statute's "aiding and abetting" provision. 15 U. S. C. § 78t(e). This provision, enforceable only by the Commission (and not by private parties), makes it unlawful to "knowingly or recklessly . . . provid[e] substantial assistance to another person" who violates the Rule. *Ibid.* . . . Lorenzo claims that imposing primary liability upon his conduct would erase or at least weaken what is otherwise a clear distinction between primary and secondary (*i.e.*, aiding and abetting) liability. He emphasizes that, under today's holding, a disseminator might be a primary offender with respect to subsection (a) of Rule 10b–5 (by employing a "scheme" to "defraud") and also secondarily liable as an aider and abettor with respect to subsection (b) (by providing substantial assistance to one who "makes" a false statement). And he refers to two cases that, in his view, argue in favor of circumscribing primary liability. . . .

We do not believe, however, that our decision creates a serious anomaly or otherwise weakens the distinction between primary and secondary liability. For one thing, it is hardly unusual for the same conduct to be a primary violation with respect to one offense and aiding and abetting with respect to another. John, for example, might sell Bill an unregistered firearm in order to help Bill rob a bank, under circumstances that make him primarily liable for the gun sale and secondarily liable for the bank robbery.

For another, the cases to which Lorenzo refers do not help his cause. Take *Central Bank*, where we held that Rule 10b–5's private right of action does not permit suits against secondary violators. 511 U. S., at 177 . . . . The holding of *Central Bank*, we have said, suggests the need for a "clean line" between conduct that constitutes a primary violation of Rule

10b–5 and conduct that amounts to a secondary violation. . . . The line we adopt today is just as administrable. Those who disseminate false statements with intent to defraud are primarily liable under Rules 10b–5(a) and (c), § 10(b). . . , even if they are secondarily liable under Rule 10b–5(b). Lorenzo suggests that classifying dissemination as a primary violation would inappropriately subject peripheral players in fraud (including him, naturally) to substantial liability. We suspect the investors who received Lorenzo's e-mails would not view the deception so favorably. And as *Central Bank* itself made clear, even a bit participant in the securities markets "may be liable as a primary violator under [Rule] 10b–5" so long as "all of the requirements for primary liability . . . are met." *Id.*, at 191 . . . .

Lorenzo's reliance on *Stoneridge* is even further afield. There, we held that private plaintiffs could not bring suit against certain securities defendants based on *undisclosed* deceptions upon which the plaintiffs could not have relied. 552 U. S., at 159 . . . . But the Commission, unlike private parties, need not show reliance in its enforcement actions. And even supposing reliance were relevant here, Lorenzo's conduct involved the direct transmission of false statements to prospective investors intended to induce reliance—far from the kind of concealed fraud at issue in *Stoneridge*.

As for Lorenzo's suggestion that those like him ought to be held secondarily liable, this offer will, far too often, prove illusory. In instances where a "maker" of a false statement does *not* violate subsection (b) of the Rule (perhaps because he lacked the necessary intent), a disseminator of those statements, even one knowingly engaged in an egregious fraud, could not be held to have violated the "aiding and abetting" statute. That is because the statute insists that there be a primary violator to whom the secondary violator provided "substantial assistance." 15 U. S. C. § 78t(e). And the latter can be "deemed to be in violation" of the provision only "to the same extent as the person to whom such assistance is provided." *Ibid.* In other words, if Acme Corp. could not be held liable under subsection (b) for a statement it made, then a knowing disseminator of those statements could not be held liable for aiding and abetting Acme under subsection (b). And if, as Lorenzo claims, the disseminator has not primarily violated other parts of Rule 10b–5, then such a fraud, whatever its intent or consequences, might escape liability altogether.

That is not what Congress intended. Rather, Congress intended to root out all manner of fraud in the securities industry. And it gave to the Commission the tools to accomplish that job.

For these reasons, the judgment of the Court of Appeals is affirmed.

So ordered.

■ JUSTICE KAVANAUGH took no part in the consideration or decision of this case.

■ JUSTICE THOMAS, with whom JUSTICE GORSUCH joins, dissenting. (dissenting opinion omitted)

8. CAUSAL RELATIONSHIP

A. LITIGATING TRANSACTION CAUSATION

Page 1048.* Add the following after "Note on Class Certification in Fraud on the Market Cases":

Goldman Sachs Grp., Inc. v. Ark. Teacher Ret. Sys.

Supreme Court of the United States.
2021 U.S. LEXIS 3391, June 21, 2021.

■ JUSTICE BARRETT delivered the opinion of the Court.

This case involves a securities-fraud class action filed by several pension funds against The Goldman Sachs Group, Inc., and three of its former executives (collectively, Goldman). Plaintiffs allege that Goldman maintained an artificially inflated stock price by making generic statements about its ability to manage conflicts—for example, "We have extensive procedures and controls that are designed to identify and address conflicts of interest." Plaintiffs say that Goldman's generic statements were false or misleading in light of several undisclosed conflicts of interest, and that once the truth about Goldman's conflicts came out, Goldman's stock price dropped and shareholders suffered losses.

. . . Plaintiffs sought to certify a class of Goldman shareholders by invoking the presumption endorsed by this Court in *Basic Inc.* v. *Levinson*, 485 U. S. 224 . . . (1988). The *Basic* presumption is premised on the theory that investors rely on the market price of a company's security, which in an efficient market incorporates all of the company's public misrepresentations. For its part, Goldman sought to defeat class certification by rebutting the *Basic* presumption through evidence that its alleged misrepresentations actually had no impact on its stock price. After determining that Goldman had failed to carry its burden of proving a lack of price impact, the District Court certified the class, and the Second Circuit affirmed. . . .

I

A . . .

This case concerns the element of reliance. The "traditional (and most direct) way" for a plaintiff to prove reliance is to show that he was aware of a defendant's misrepresentation and engaged in a transaction based on that misrepresentation. *Ibid.* (internal quotation marks omitted). In *Basic*, however, we held that a plaintiff may also invoke a

---

rebuttable presumption of reliance based on the fraud-on-the-market theory. 485 U. S., at 241–247 . . . .

The "fundamental premise" of the fraud-on-the-market theory underlying *Basic*'s presumption is "that an investor presumptively relies on a misrepresentation so long as it was reflected in the market price at the time of his transaction." *Erica P. John Fund, Inc. v. Halliburton Co.*, 563 U. S. 804, 813 . . . (2011). To invoke the *Basic* presumption, a plaintiff must prove: (1) that the alleged misrepresentation was publicly known; (2) that it was material; (3) that the stock traded in an efficient market; and (4) that the plaintiff traded the stock between the time the misrepresentation was made and when the truth was revealed. *Halliburton II*, 573 U. S., at 268 . . . . The defendant may then rebut the presumption through "[a]ny showing that severs the link between the alleged misrepresentation and either the price received (or paid) by the plaintiff, or his decision to trade at a fair market price." *Basic*, 485 U. S., at 248 . . . .

Although the *Basic* presumption "can be invoked by any Rule 10b–5 plaintiff," it has "particular significance in securities-fraud class actions." *Amgen Inc. v. Connecticut Retirement Plans and Trust Funds*, 568 U. S. 455 . . . (2013). The presumption allows class-action plaintiffs to prove reliance through evidence common to the class. That in turn makes it easier for plaintiffs to establish the predominance requirement of Federal Rule of Civil Procedure 23, which requires that "questions of law or fact common to class members predominate" over individualized issues. Fed. Rule Civ. Proc. 23(b)(3). Indeed, without the *Basic* presumption, individualized issues of reliance ordinarily would defeat predominance and "preclude certification" of a securities-fraud class action. *Amgen*, 568 U. S., at 462–463 . . . .

As a result, class-action plaintiffs must prove the *Basic* prerequisites before class certification—with one exception. In *Amgen*, we held that materiality should be left to the merits stage because it does not bear on Rule 23's predominance requirement. 568 U. S., at 466–468 . . . . The remaining *Basic* prerequisites—publicity, market efficiency, and market timing—"must be satisfied" by plaintiffs "before class certification." *Halliburton II*, 573 U. S., at 276 . . . .

Satisfying those prerequisites, however, does not guarantee class certification. We held in *Halliburton II* that defendants may rebut the *Basic* presumption at class certification by showing "that an alleged misrepresentation did not actually affect the market price of the stock." *Id.*, at 284, 134 S. Ct. 2398, 189 L. Ed. 2d 339. If a misrepresentation had no price impact, then *Basic*'s fundamental premise "completely collapses, rendering class certification inappropriate." *Id.*, at 283, 134 S. Ct. 2398, 189 L. Ed. 2d 339.

B . . .

The specific theory of securities fraud that Plaintiffs allege is known as inflation maintenance. Under this theory, a misrepresentation causes a stock price "to *remain* inflated by preventing preexisting inflation from dissipating from the stock price." *FindWhat Investor Group v. FindWhat.com*, 658 F. 3d 1282, 1315 (CA11 2011).[1]

Plaintiffs allege here that between 2006 and 2010, Goldman maintained an inflated stock price by making repeated misrepresentations about its conflict-of-interest policies and business practices. The alleged misrepresentations are generic statements from Goldman's SEC filings and annual reports, including the following:

- "We have extensive procedures and controls that are designed to identify and address conflicts of interest." App. 216 (emphasis and boldface deleted).

- "Our clients' interests always come first." *Id.*, at 162 (same).

- "Integrity and honesty are at the heart of our business." *Id.*, at 163 (same).

According to Plaintiffs, these statements were false or misleading—and caused Goldman's stock to trade at artificially inflated levels—because Goldman had in fact engaged in several allegedly conflicted transactions without disclosing the conflicts. Plaintiffs further allege that once the market learned the truth about Goldman's conflicts from a Government enforcement action and subsequent news reports, the inflation in Goldman's stock price dissipated, causing the price to drop and shareholders to suffer losses.

After Goldman unsuccessfully moved to dismiss the case, Plaintiffs moved to certify the class, invoking the *Basic* presumption. In response, Goldman sought to rebut the *Basic* presumption by proving a lack of price impact. Both parties submitted extensive expert testimony on the issue. . . .

We granted certiorari. 592 U. S. ___, 141 S. Ct. 950, 208 L. Ed. 2d 488 (2020).

II

Goldman argues that the Second Circuit erred in two respects: first, by concluding that the generic nature of alleged misrepresentations is irrelevant to the price impact question; and second, by placing the burden of persuasion on Goldman to prove a lack of price impact. We address these arguments in turn.

---

[1]   Although some Courts of Appeals have approved the inflation-maintenance theory, this Court has expressed no view on its validity or its contours. We need not and do not do so in this case.

A

1

On the first question—whether the generic nature of a misrepresentation is relevant to price impact—the parties' dispute has largely evaporated. Plaintiffs now concede that the generic nature of an alleged misrepresentation often will be important evidence of price impact because, as a rule of thumb, "a more-general statement will affect a security's price less than a more-specific statement on the same question." Brief for Respondents 15 . . . . The parties further agree that courts may consider expert testimony and use their common sense in assessing whether a generic misrepresentation had a price impact. . . . And they likewise agree that courts may assess the generic nature of a misrepresentation at class certification even though it also may be relevant to materiality, which *Amgen* reserves for the merits. See *id.*, at 23, 65.

We share the parties' view. In assessing price impact at class certification, courts " 'should be open to *all* probative evidence on that question—qualitative as well as quantitative—aided by a good dose of common sense.' " *In re Allstate Corp. Securities Litig.*, 966 F. 3d 595, 613, n. 6 (CA7 2020) (quoting Langevoort, Judgment Day for Fraud-on-the-Market: Reflection on *Amgen* and the Second Coming of *Halliburton*, 57 Ariz. L. Rev. 37, 56 (2015); emphasis added). . . . And under *Halliburton II*, a court cannot conclude that Rule 23's requirements are satisfied without considering *all* evidence relevant to price impact. See 573 U. S., at 284, 134 S. Ct. 2398, 189 L. Ed. 2d 339.[2]

The generic nature of a misrepresentation often will be important evidence of a lack of price impact, particularly in cases proceeding under the inflation-maintenance theory. Under that theory, price impact is the amount of price inflation maintained by an alleged misrepresentation—in other words, the amount that the stock's price would have fallen "without the false statement." *Glickenhaus & Co. v. Household Int'l, Inc.*, 787 F. 3d 408, 415 (CA7 2020). Plaintiffs typically try to prove the amount of inflation indirectly: They point to a negative disclosure about a company and an associated drop in its stock price; allege that the disclosure corrected an earlier misrepresentation; and then claim that the price drop is equal to the amount of inflation maintained by the earlier misrepresentation. See, *e.g.*, *id.*, at 413–417; *In re Vivendi, S.A. Securities Litig.*, 838 F. 3d 223, 233–237, 253–259 (CA2 2016).

But that final inference—that the back-end price drop equals front-end inflation—starts to break down when there is a mismatch between

---

[2]   We recognize that materiality and price impact are overlapping concepts and that the evidence relevant to one will almost always be relevant to the other. But "a district court may not use the overlap to refuse to consider the evidence." *In re Allstate*, 966 F. 3d, at 608. Instead, the district court must use the evidence to decide the price impact issue "while resisting the temptation to draw what may be obvious inferences for the closely related issues that must be left for the merits, including materiality." *Id.*, at 609.

the contents of the misrepresentation and the corrective disclosure. That may occur when the earlier misrepresentation is generic (*e.g.*, "we have faith in our business model") and the later corrective disclosure is specific (*e.g.*, "our fourth quarter earnings did not meet expectations"). Under those circumstances, it is less likely that the specific disclosure actually corrected the generic misrepresentation, which means that there is less reason to infer front-end price inflation—that is, price impact—from the back-end price drop.

2

The parties do not dispute any of this. They disagree only about whether the Second Circuit properly considered the generic nature of Goldman's alleged misrepresentations. Because the Second Circuit's opinions leave us with sufficient doubt on this score, we remand for further consideration. On remand, the Second Circuit must take into account *all* record evidence relevant to price impact, regardless whether that evidence overlaps with materiality or any other merits issue.

B

Goldman also argues that the Second Circuit erred by requiring Goldman, rather than Plaintiffs, to bear the burden of persuasion on price impact at class certification. Goldman relies exclusively on Federal Rule of Evidence 301, which provides in full:

> "In a civil case, unless a federal statute or these rules provide otherwise, the party against whom a presumption is directed has the burden of producing evidence to rebut the presumption. But this rule does not shift the burden of persuasion, which remains on the party who had it originally."

According to Goldman, Rule 301 applies to the *Basic* presumption at class certification, and, as a result, a plaintiff's satisfaction of the *Basic* prerequisites shifts only the burden of *production* to the defendant. Once a defendant discharges that burden by producing any competent evidence of a lack of price impact, Goldman says, the *Basic* presumption is rebutted and the plaintiff must carry the burden of *persuasion* to show price impact.

We disagree. We have held that Rule 301 "in no way restricts the authority of a court . . . to change the customary burdens of persuasion" pursuant to a federal statute. *NLRB v. Transportation Management Corp.*, 462 U. S. 393, 404, n. 7 . . . (1983). And we have at times exercised that authority to reassign the burden of persuasion to the defendant upon a prima facie showing by the plaintiff. See, *e.g.*, *Teamsters v. United States*, 431 U. S. 324, 359 . . . (1977) . . . .

. . . So the threshold question here is not whether we have the authority to assign defendants the burden of persuasion to prove a lack of price impact, but instead whether we already exercised that authority in establishing the *Basic* framework pursuant to the securities laws. We conclude that *Basic* and *Halliburton II* did just that.

Basic held that defendants may rebut the presumption of reliance if they "*show* that the misrepresentation *in fact* did not lead to a distortion of price." 485 U. S., at 248 . . . (emphasis added). To do so, *Basic* said, defendants may make "[a]ny *showing* that *severs the link* between the alleged misrepresentation and . . . the price received (or paid) by the plaintiff." *Ibid.* (emphasis added). Similarly, *Halliburton II* held that defendants may rebut the *Basic* presumption at class certification "by *showing* . . . that the particular misrepresentation at issue did not affect the stock's market price." 573 U. S., at 279 . . . (emphasis added).

Goldman and JUSTICE GORSUCH argue that these references to a defendant's "showing" refer to the defendant's burden of production. . . . (dissenting opinion) (hereinafter the dissent). On this reading, *Basic* and *Halliburton II* require a defendant merely to offer "evidence that, if believed, would support a finding" of a lack of price impact. . . . But *Basic* and *Halliburton II* plainly require more: The defendant must "in fact" "seve[r] the link" between a misrepresentation and the price paid by the plaintiff—and a defendant's mere production of *some* evidence relevant to price impact would rarely accomplish that feat.[4]

Accepting Goldman and the dissent's argument would also effectively negate *Halliburton II* 's holding that plaintiffs need not directly prove price impact in order to invoke the *Basic* presumption. 573 U. S., at 278–279 . . . . If, as they urge, the defendant could defeat *Basic's* presumption by introducing *any* competent evidence of a lack of price impact—including, for example, the generic nature of the alleged misrepresentations—then the plaintiff would end up with the burden of directly proving price impact in almost every case. And that would be nearly indistinguishable from the regime that *Halliburton II* rejected.

Thus, the best reading of our precedents . . . is that the defendant bears the burden of persuasion to prove a lack of price impact. See *Waggoner v. Barclays PLC*, 875 F. 3d 79, 99–104 (CA2 2017) ("the phrase '[a]ny showing that severs the link' aligns more logically with imposing a burden of persuasion rather than a burden of production") . . . .We likewise agree with the Courts of Appeals that the defendant must carry that burden by a preponderance of the evidence. See *Waggoner*, 875 F. 3d, at 99; *In re Allstate*, 966 F. 3d, at 610.

Although the defendant bears the burden of persuasion, the allocation of the burden is unlikely to make much difference on the ground. In most securities-fraud class actions, as in this one, the plaintiffs and defendants submit competing expert evidence on price impact. The district court's task is simply to assess all the evidence of price impact—direct and indirect—and determine whether it is more likely than not that the alleged misrepresentations had a price impact.

---

[4]   The dissent points out that, as a general rule, presumptions shift only the burden of production. *Post*, at 2–4. We don't disagree, but we read *Basic* and *Halliburton II* as a clear departure from that general rule.

The defendant's burden of persuasion will have bite only when the court finds the evidence in equipoise—a situation that should rarely arise. . . .

The Second Circuit correctly placed the burden of proving a lack of price impact on Goldman. But because it is unclear whether the Second Circuit properly considered the generic nature of Goldman's alleged misrepresentations in reviewing the District Court's price impact determination, we vacate the judgment of the Second Circuit and remand the case for further proceedings consistent with this opinion.

■ JUSTICE SOTOMAYOR, concurring in part and dissenting in part.

I agree with the Court's answers to the questions presented, and I accordingly join Parts I, II-A-1, and II-B of the Court's opinion. . . .

I do not, however, join the Court's judgment to vacate and remand because I believe the Second Circuit "properly considered the generic nature of Goldman's alleged misrepresentations." . . .

■ JUSTICE GORSUCH, with whom JUSTICE THOMAS and JUSTICE ALITO join, concurring in part and dissenting in part.

I join all but Part II-B of the Court's opinion. There, the Court holds that the defendant, rather than the plaintiff, "bear[s] the burden of persuasion on price impact." Respectfully, I disagree. . . .

Before us, the only meaningful dispute concerns what burden a defendant bears when it comes to rebutting the *Basic* presumption. Does the defendant carry only a burden of *production*, or does the defendant sometimes carry a burden of *persuasion*? In my view, only a burden of production is involved.

Start with what we have said about presumptions like *Basic*'s. This Court has long recognized that a " ' "presumption" properly used refers only to a device for allocating the production burden.' " *Texas Dept. of Community Affairs v. Burdine*, 450 U. S. 248, 255, n. 8 . . . (1981). Throughout the law, courts have sometimes created presumptions to help plaintiffs prove their cases when direct evidence can be hard to come by. See *Basic*, 485 U. S., at 245 . . . . These presumptions operate by allowing the plaintiff to prove only certain specified "predicate fact[s]" at the outset. *St. Mary's Honor Center v. Hicks*, 509 U. S. 502, 506 . . . (1993). If the plaintiff does so, an inference or "presumption" arises that the plaintiff has met its burden of persuasion, at least "in the absence" of some competing "explanation." *Ibid.* (internal quotation marks omitted). At that point, the defendant bears a burden of production to present evidence that, if "taken as true," would "permit the conclusion" that the presumption in the plaintiff's favor is mistaken. *Id.*, at 509 . . . (emphasis deleted). If the defendant produces such evidence, the presumption "drops from the case." *Id.*, at 507 . . . . "[T]he trier of fact" then "proceeds to decide the ultimate question." *Id.*, at 511 . . . . Throughout this whole back-and-forth process, the burden of persuasion never shifts: The "plaintiff at all times bears the ultimate burden of persuasion" to prove all aspects of its cause of action. *Ibid.* (internal quotation marks omitted). . . .

The Court disputes none of this. It does not even try to defend on the merits its unusual suggestion that the *defendant* carries some burden of persuasion in a *plaintiff's* claim for securities fraud. Instead, the Court contends only that precedent ties our hands.

Primarily, the Court points to a single clause in a single sentence in *Basic* observing that a defendant may rebut the presumption of reliance with "[a]ny showing that severs the link between the alleged misrepresentation" and the stock price. . . . The Court then splices that clause together with another clause in a preceding sentence explaining that, before *Basic*, lower courts had said a defendant rebuts the fraud on the market presumption by showing "that the misrepresentation in fact did not lead to a distortion of price." . . .

That much does not follow either. Like *Basic*, *Halliburton II* concerned what facts a plaintiff must produce to *generate* a presumption of reliance. This case is about what defendants must do to *rebut* that presumption. Deciding one does not resolve the other. To say these issues are "indistinguishable" is to miss the entire point of a presumption: It allows the plaintiff to state a prima facie case based on inference and requires the defendant to bear the burden of producing evidence in response; once the defendant does so, the presumption has served its purpose and drops from the case. At that point, the factfinder now has the benefit of evidence from both sides and must decide the case with reference to the plaintiff's burden of persuasion. Nothing in *Halliburton II* suggests a departure from these principles, let alone that some burden of persuasion secretly shifts to the defendant in a plaintiff's claim for securities fraud. To the contrary, that decision arose in the class certification context and expressly *reaffirmed* that "[t]he *Basic* presumption does not relieve plaintiffs of the burden of proving" they have satisfied "the predominance requirement of Rule 23(b)(3)." 573 U. S., at 276 . . . .

Perhaps recognizing the incongruity of its conclusion, the Court goes out of its way to downplay its significance. We're told that "on the ground" today's holding "is unlikely to make much difference" because "[i]n most securities-fraud class actions . . . the plaintiffs and defendants submit competing expert evidence on price impact." *Ante*, at 12. And in cases like these, "[t]he district court's task," according to the Court, "is simply to assess all the evidence of price impact" and "determine whether it is more likely than not that the alleged misrepresentations had a price impact." *Ibid.*

This is a curious disavowal. Obviously, the Court thinks the issue important enough to spend the time and effort to rejigger the burden of persuasion. Now, though, it says none of this matters because most cases come down to a dispute over evidence of price impact irrespective of the presumption. The Court's suggestion that the burden of persuasion will "rarely" make a "difference" misses the point too. The whole reason we allocate the burden of persuasion is to resolve close cases by providing a tie breaker where the burden *does* make a difference. That close cases may not be common ones is no justification for indifference about how the law resolves them.

Respectfully, I dissent.

CHAPTER 13

INSIDER TRADING

2. THE FEDERAL DISCLOSE OR ABSTAIN REQUIREMENT

Page 1137.* Add the following at the end of Section 2:

NOTE ON OTHER BASES FOR CRIMINAL PROSECUTIONS OF
INSIDER TRADING

In addition to Rule 10b–5 and Rule 14e–3, the government has a panoply of
provisions it can employ to prosecute *criminally* insiders, tippers and tippees
who trade on material non-public information. Indeed, as illustrated in
United States v. Blaszczak, 947 F.3d 19 (2nd Cir. 2019), these provisions can
be less demanding on the prosecutor than Rule 10b–5. Huber and Olan
garnered substantial profits for their employer (a hedge fund) by trading on
material non-public information that Blaszczak leached from Worrall, his
former colleague at the Centers for Medicare & Medicaid Services (CMMS).
The information pertained to the federal government's plans to slash
Medicare and Medicaid reimbursement rates for various medical procedures.
Huber and Olan, upon receiving the tip, initiated short sales of various
health care providers on behalf of their employer. The jury returned non-
guilty verdicts with respect to the Rule 10b–5 charges because there was not
sufficient evidence that Worrall, the tipper, received a personal benefit as a
result of his selective disclosures to Blaszczak. However, the jury convicted
all the defendants for Wire Fraud, 18 U.S.C. § 1343 and for violating the
Sarbanes-Oxley Act Securities Fraud, 18 U.S.C. § 1348. *Blaszczak* affirmed
the trial convictions under each of these provisions. With respect to the
former, *Blaszczak* followed the precedent of *Carpenter v. United States*, 484
U.S. 19 (1987), holding that employer has a property right in its confidential
information so that the knowing unauthorized use of such confidential
information is itself a violation without the need to establish any further
violation by the breaching employee. Even more sweeping is *Blaszczak's*
reasoning that Section 1348 was enacted "in large part to overcome technical
legal requirements of" Rule 10b–5. *Id.* at 32. Hence, both provisions of Title
18 do not require the government to establish a *Dirks/Salman* personal-
benefit test.

The government's victory, however, was short lived. *United States v.
Blaszczak*, 141 S.Ct. 1040 (2021), remanded the case to the Second Circuit to
reconsider whether, in light of *Kelly v. United States*, 140 U.S. 1565 (2020),
there was a property right that Blaszczak had violated by his wrongful
tipping. *Kelly* arose from the infamous "BridgeGate" where state officials
punished out of political concerns some local politicians by disrupting traffic
into New York City. *Kelly* held that confidential information abused by the
defendants in that case was not the kind of property covered by the statutes;

---

*   The bottom of page 862 in the Condensed Edition.

this reasoning prompted the Department of Justice to question whether the information Blaszczak misused that came from the CMMS, a *public* agency, was also beyond the scope of the statute. It remains an open question whether this will be the view of the Second Circuit and, even if the court did so hold, whether *Kelly* is limited to abuses of confidential information in the *public* sector.

CHAPTER 14

SHAREHOLDER SUITS

6. THE DEMAND REQUIREMENT

Page 1222.* Insert the following before *Del. County Employees Ret. Fund v. Sanchez*:

NOTE ON DELAWARE'S "REFINED" DEMAND FUTILITY TEST

In *United Food & Commercial Workers Union v. Zuckerberg*, 62 A.3d 1034 (Del. 2021), the Delaware Supreme Court refined its approach to considering whether a demand is excused that combined elements from *Aronson v. Lewis* and *Rales v. Blasband* so as to create a single three-part demand futility test. The Court acknowledged that significant changes in Delaware law—notably, the enactment of DGCL § 102(b)(7)—since *Aronson* was decided had "eroded the ground upon which [the *Aronson*] framework rested" and, as a result, justified refining the test to "refocus" the inquiry "on the decision regarding the litigation demand, rather than the decision being challenged." The Supreme Court noted that the refined standard is consistent with *Aronson*, *Rales*, and their progeny, and cases properly applying those holdings remain good law.

In an earlier class action, Facebook stockholders had claimed that Facebook's board breached its fiduciary duties by approving and pursuing a reclassification of Facebook's shares that would have enabled Mark Zuckerberg to retain voting control of the company despite donating a significant amount of stock to charities. The reclassification was later withdrawn, and a settlement was reached with the complaining shareholders. Following the settlement, another Facebook stockholder—the United Food and Commercial Workers Union and Participating Food Industry Employers Tri-State Pension Fund ("Tri-State")—filed a derivative complaint in the Chancery Court. This new action sought compensation for the money Facebook spent in connection with the prior class action. Tri-State did not make a litigation demand on Facebook's board. Instead, Tri-State pleaded that demand was futile because the board's negotiation and approval of the reclassification was not a valid exercise of its business judgment and because a majority of the directors were beholden to Zuckerberg.

Aronson set forth that demand is excused as futile if the complaint alleges particularized facts that raise a reasonable doubt that (1) the directors are disinterested and independent or (2) the challenged transaction was otherwise "the product of a valid business judgment." Because Facebook's charter contained a Section 102(b)(7) clause, the Facebook board faced no risk of personal liability from Tri-State's breach-of-care allegations.

---

*   Page 922 in the Concise Edition.

A key question the Chancery Court addressed was whether Tri-State's demand-futility allegations could rely on exculpated care violations to establish that demand was futile under the second prong of the *Aronson* test—there being a reasonable doubt "the challenged transaction was otherwise the product of a valid exercise of business judgment." The Supreme Court agreed with the Chancery Court that exculpated care claims do not excuse demand because the second prong of *Aronson* focuses on whether a director faces a substantial likelihood of liability, notwithstanding text in the second prong that focused on the propriety of the "challenged transaction." The Supreme Court held that *Aronson*'s overarching concern was (quoting from *Aronson*) less on the decision being challenged and more on whether the directors on the demand board "cannot be considered proper persons to conduct litigation on behalf of the corporation" because they "are under an influence which sterilizes their discretion." The Supreme Court noted:

> The purpose of the demand futility analysis is to assess whether the board should be deprived of its decision-making authority because there is reason to doubt that the directors would be able to bring their impartial business judgment to bear on a litigation demand. That is a different consideration than whether the derivative claim is strong or weak because the challenged transaction is likely to pass or fail the applicable standard of review. It is helpful to keep those inquiries separate. And the Court of Chancery's three-part test is particularly helpful where, like here, board turnover and director abstention make it difficult to apply the *Aronson* test as written.

Going forward, the Supreme Court stated, "courts should ask the following three questions on a director-by-director basis when evaluating allegations of demand futility:

- whether the director received a material personal benefit from the alleged misconduct that is the subject of the litigation demand;

- whether the director faces a substantial likelihood of liability on any of the claims that would be the subject of the litigation demand; and

- whether the director lacks independence from someone who received a material personal benefit from the alleged misconduct that would be the subject of the litigation demand or who would face a substantial likelihood of liability on any of the claims that are the subject of the litigation demand.

If the answer to any of the questions is "yes" for at least half of the members of the demand board, then demand is excused as futile."

This refined three-part test applies to a court's assessment of any claim that demand would be futile. It is no longer necessary to determine whether the *Aronson* test or the *Rales* test governs a complaint's demand-futility allegations.

Page 1225.* Add the following at the beginning of "Notes on Independence":

More recently, *Marchand v. Barnhill*, 212 A.3d 305 (Del. 2018), held that W.J. Rankin, the firm's former chief financial officer, was not sufficiently independent in the calculation whether demand should be excused in a derivative suit against Paul Kruse. The court emphasized that the facts supported a belief that much of Rankin's successful 28-year career with the firm was attributable to the nurturing hand of Ed Kruse, the derivative suit defendant's father, for whom he initially served as an administrative assistant, by whom he was later promoted to the firm's CFO (a position he retired from a few months before the derivative suit was filed), and with whose support he ultimately served on the board for 15 years. Also, the Kruse family spearheaded a campaign to fund a large donation to a local university in the name of Rankin with the consequential effect that a new agricultural facility was named after him. The court further reasoned that Rankin's lack of independence was unaffected by Rankin recently voting in favor of a failed resolution that would have barred Paul Kruse from being the board's chair while also serving as its CEO.

Page 1229. Insert the following at the bottom of the page:

6. Excusing Demand in Caremark/*Oversight Claims.* Recall that *Caremark,* as refined by *Stone,* imposes director liability if the plaintiff establishes the directors "utterly failed to implement any reporting or information system or controls; or . . . having implemented such a system or controls, consciously failed to monitor or oversee its operations thus disabling themselves from being informed of risks or problems requiring their attention." *Stone v. Ritter*, 911 A.2d 362, 370 (Del. 2006). In such oversight claims, what excuses a demand on the board of directors? In such suits, the facts do not raise questions of self-dealing by the directors or that they are under the influence of a wrongdoer. Excusing demand requires particularized facts that directors face a substantial likelihood of liability for their breach of their oversight duties. *Hughes v. Hu*, 2020 Del. Ch. LEXIS 162 (Del. Ch. Apr. 27, 2020), found sufficient allegations of facts to support excusing demand where the facts alleged showed that even though the company had an audit committee, the committee met only sporadically and deliberated in a perfunctory manner or the committee had clear notice of serious accounting irregularities and chose to ignore them. In meeting this pleading requirement, consider *Teamsters Local 443 Health Servs. & Ins. Plan v. Chou*, 2020 Del. Ch. LEXIS 274 (Del. Ch. Aug. 24, 2020)("when a company operates in an environment where externally imposed regulations govern its mission critical operations, the board's oversight function must be more rigorously exercised").

---

*   Page 925 at the end of *Sanchez* in Section 5 of the Condensed Edition.

13. PRIVATE ORDERING AND SHAREHOLDER SUITS

Page 1305.* Add the following to the end of the text:

In *Salzberg v. Sciabacucchi*, 227 A.3d 102 (Del. 2020), the Delaware Supreme Court made its most striking embrace of the scope of private ordering with potentially far-reaching impact on federalism. The dispute focused on the validity of so-called federal-forum provisions (FFP) that many companies going public include in their articles of incorporation. For example, ROKU's FFP provides:

> Unless the Company consents in writing to the selection of an alternative forum, the federal district courts of the United States of America shall be the exclusive forum for the resolution of any complaint asserting a cause of action arising under the Securities Act of 1933. Any person or entity purchasing or otherwise acquiring any interest in any security of [the Company] shall be deemed to have notice of and consented to [this provision].

The impetus for PPFs among companies going public is that the companies and officers are subject to liability under the Federal Securities Act of 1933 if their offering materials are materially misleading and the '33 Act expressly authorizes suits in either federal or state court. Alarm over such suits follows studies reporting that, consistent with more permissive state procedural rules on matters such as pleading and availability of discovery, dismissal rates in state courts are significantly below those in federal courts, and settlements occur in about 80 percent of all the state filings even if the parallel federal case has been dismissed. *See e.g.,* Klausner, Hegland, LeVine & Shin, State Section 11 Litigation in the Post-*Cyan* Environment (Despite *Sciabacucchi*), 75 Bus. Law. 1769 (2020). In the face of a noticeable increase in '33 Act suits in state courts, many corporations, such as Roku, inserted PPF provisions into their articles of incorporation.

Salzberg involved several corporations, directors and officers sued under in the Delaware Chancery Court under the '33 Act who invoked their firm's FFP in an effort to lodge the litigation in a federal forum. The Chancery Court held the FFP provision did not involve "internal affairs" of the company and hence were not valid. The Delaware Supreme Court reversed, reasoning:

> The analysis must begin with the text of Section 102, the provision of the Delaware General Corporation Law ("DGCL") governing the matters contained in a corporation's certificate of incorporation. . . .

---

*   Page 982 in Section 12 of the Condensed Edition.

Section 102(b)(1) provides:

> (b) In addition to the matters required to be set forth in the certificate of incorporation by subsection (a) of this section, the certificate of incorporation may also contain any or all of the following matters: (1) Any provision for the management of the business and for the conduct of the affairs of the corporation, and any provision creating, defining, limiting and regulating the powers of the corporation, the directors, and the stockholders, or any class of the stockholders, or the governing body, members, or any class or group of members of a nonstock corporation; if such provisions are not contrary to the laws of this State. Any provision which is required or permitted by any section of this chapter to be stated in the bylaws may instead be stated in the certificate of incorporation . . .

Thus, Section 102(b)(1) authorizes two broad types of provisions:

> *any* provision for the management of the business and for the conduct of the affairs of the corporation,

and

> *any* provision creating, defining, limiting and regulating the powers of the corporation, the directors, and the stockholders, or any class of the stockholders, . . . if such provisions are not contrary to the laws of this State.

An FFP could easily fall within either of these broad categories, and thus, is facially valid. FFPs involve a type of securities claim related to the management of litigation arising out of the Board's disclosures to current and prospective stockholders in connection with an IPO or secondary offering. The drafting, reviewing, and filing of registration statements by a corporation and its directors is an important aspect of a corporation's management of its business and affairs and of its relationship with its stockholders. This Court has viewed the overlap of federal and state law in the disclosure area as "historic," "compatible," and "complimentary." Accordingly, a bylaw that seeks to regulate the forum in which such "intra-corporate" litigation can occur is a provision that addresses the "management of the business" and the "conduct of the affairs of the corporation," and is, thus, facially valid under Section 102(b)(1).

In its opinion, the court goes to great lengths to develop the view that "intra-corporate matters" is broader than "internal affairs." Part of the impetus for this distinction is Section 115 of the Delaware General Corporation Law, as discussed above, which prohibits article and bylaw provisions that would *prevent* corporate suits in Delaware courts.

Query, does premising the validity of FFPs on their not involving "internal affairs" rob the FFP of some of its force when the validity of the FFP is contested in a sister state court? This problem arises because the traditional choice of law rule for corporate law is to apply the law of the state of incorporation, but this rule applies only to matters involving internal affairs. Can the sister state therefore apply its own law in deciding the validity of a FFP invoked by a Delaware corporation targeted in '33 Act litigation? *Salzberg* reasoned that such a challenge would be guided by contractual principles so that the articles of incorporation frames the relationship of shareholders and the corporation, and that contract law would support the efficacy of the FFP. *See also,* Joseph A. Grundfest, The Limits of Delaware Corporate Law: Internal Affairs, Federal Forum Provisions, and *Sciabacucchi*, 75 Bus. L. 1319 (2020).

Does *Salzberg* support a provision calling for arbitration of all shareholder disputes against the corporation, its officers and directors under state law or federal securities laws? In this regard, consider the No-Action Letter granted Johnson & Johnson set forth in Chapter 6 addressing such a proposal for arbitration of securities fraud suits against the company. Consider further *Salzberg's* reference to this topic:

> Much of the opposition to FFPs seems to be based upon a concern that if upheld, the "next move" might be forum provisions that require arbitration of internal corporate claims. Such provisions, at least from our state law perspective, would violate Section 115 which provides that, "no provision of the certificate of incorporation or the bylaws may prohibit bringing such claims in the courts of this state." 8 *Del. C.* § 115; *see* Del. S.B. 75 syn. ("Section 115 does not address the validity of a provision of the certificate of incorporation or bylaws that selects a forum other than the Delaware courts as an additional forum in which internal corporate claims may be brought, but it invalidates such a provision selecting the courts in a different State, *or an arbitral forum*, if it would preclude litigating such claims in the Delaware courts." (emphasis added)).

227 A.3d at 137 n. 169. Does a securities law claim involve internal affairs? If not, is arbitration of such a claim addressed by Section 115 of the Delaware statute?

Vigorous challenges to the validity of forum selection clauses (FSCs) that direct lawsuits to state court have occurred in cases where the complaints raise claims under the federal securities laws. The results in these suits before federal courts are mixed. *Compare* Lee v. Fisher, 34 F.4th 777 (9th Cir. 2022)(suit alleging violation of Section 14(a) and Rule 14a–9, for which the Exchange Act provides exclusive jurisdiction is in the federal courts, nonetheless dismissed from federal court pursuant to FSC on the reasoning that Supreme Court precedent upholds the validity of choice of law provisions as means of addressing *forum non conveniens* considerations) *with* Seafarers Pension Plan v. Bradway, 23 F.4th 714 (7th Cir. 2022)(federal securities claim such as Rule 14a–9 is not within the intended scope of Delaware provisions authorizing FSCs and are distinguishable from cases in which the Supreme Court has upheld choice of forum provisions).

FSCs that limit actions under the federal securities laws to the federal district courts have been more successful in the state courts. Following *Salzberg*, several California state courts have dismissed claims against issuers and their directors and officers asserted under the Securities Act of 1933. And, recently, a New York court joined this line of cases in *Hook v. Casa Systems, Inc.*, No. 654548/2019, 2021 WL 3884063 (N.Y. Sup. Ct. Aug. 30, 2021), which enforced the issuer's FSC and dismissed Securities Act claims against the issuer, underwriters, and alleged control person defendants. The court held that, because Casa Systems is a Delaware corporation, the internal affairs doctrine applied and the FSC was enforceable under the holding in *Salzberg*. The court also reasoned that, even if the internal affairs doctrine did not apply, the outcome would not change if New York law applied because an FSC is presumptively valid under New York law absent proof that its enforcement would be unreasonable and unjust or that the clause is invalid due to fraud, and plaintiff made no such showing. The court rejected plaintiff's constitutional arguments, holding that the FSC did not violate the Supremacy Clause or the Commerce Clause.

CHAPTER 15

CORPORATE COMBINATIONS, TENDER OFFERS AND DEFENDING CONTROL

1. CORPORATE COMBINATIONS

B. THE APPRAISAL REMEDY

Page 1318.* Add the following after current note 5:

6. Private Ordering and the Appraisal Remedy. Is an agreement among shareholders waiving their appraisal remedy enforceable? *Manti Holdings, LLC v. Authentix Acquisition Co.*, 261 A.3d 2021 (Del. 2021), upheld such arrangement among sophisticated stockholders. As part of a 2008 acquisition transaction whereby The Carlyle Group gained control of Authentix, Inc., the former shareholders of Authentix, Inc. agreed: "In the event ... a company sale is approved by the Board and ... the Carlyle Majority, each Other Holder shall consent to and raise no objection against such transaction ..., and ... [shall] refrain from the exercise of appraisal rights with respect to such transaction." To raise additional capital, preferred shares were issued pro rata among the existing stockholders, i.e., the minority holders and Carlyle. In 2017, Authentix, Inc. was acquired by a third party on terms that provided little to no compensation to its common stockholders so that nearly all the consideration was paid to the preferred stockholders. The minority holders of the common shares sued for appraisal.

In denying the minority's claim for appraisal, the *Manti Holdings* majority reasoned:

> [T]he crux of Petitioners' argument ... [is that] appraisal rights are core characteristics of the corporate entity that provides basic protections to investors; as such they cannot be waived....

> We acknowledge that the availability of appraisal rights might theoretically discourage attempts to pay minority stockholders less than fair value for their cancelled stock. Nonetheless, the focus of an appraisal proceeding is paying fair value for the petitioner's stock, not policing or preserving the ability of stockholders to participate in corporate governance. Granting stockholders the individual right to demand fair value does not prohibit stockholders from bargaining away that individual right in exchange for valuable consideration. And while the availability of appraisal rights may deter some unfair transactions at the margins, we are unconvinced that appraisal claims play a sufficiently important

---

role in regulating the balance of power between corporate constituencies to forbid sophisticated and informed stockholders from freely agreeing to an *ex ante* waiver of their appraisal rights under a stockholders agreement in exchange for consideration.

Id. at 1223–34.

In a vigorous dissent, Justice Valihura argued that appraisal rights are so fundamental that any modification must occur within the corporate charter and even if so waived the waiver may not be valid since appraisal rights could be mandatory in light of the use of the mandatory "shall" command in Section 262 of the Delaware statute setting forth the remedy. The dissent raises a broader concern:

> There are some valid policy concerns with using stockholder agreements to effect *ex ante* waivers of appraisal rights for common stockholders. For example, some commentators have pointed out the dangers of "stealth governance" and have argued that "using shareholder agreements for corporate governance . . . sacrifices critical corporate law values." . . . [Fisch, Stealth Governance: Shareholder Agreements and Private Ordering (2021)]. The scope of these stockholder agreements now includes (putative) restrictions or waivers of inspection rights, appraisal rights and fiduciary duties of directors. No doubt, the sophisticated parties entering into these agreements have found them to be beneficial. Stockholder agreements may offer venture capital funded start-ups flexibility versus complying with the formalities of charters or bylaws. And unlike charters, they are not public documents filed with the Secretary of State. But restrictions or elimination of important stockholder rights such as inspection, appraisal, election rights and fiduciary duties may minimize accountability of the Board and upset the delicate balance of power that the General Assembly and courts have attempted to maintain among a Delaware corporation's constituencies.

Id. at 1241–43.

Page 1328.* Insert the following after the first full paragraph:

Delaware courts continue to give a good deal of deference to the deal price, and in appropriate cases hold that fair value is the deal price. Most recently, the Delaware Supreme Court identified the following as *among* indicia of the reliability of the sales process so that the deal price is the best indicator of fair value: 1) the merger was an arm's length transaction, 2) the board did not labor under any conflicts of interest, 3) the buyer conducted due diligence and received confidential information about the seller's value, 4) the seller negotiated multiple price increases, and 5) no bidders emerged during the post-signing period. *Brigade Leveraged Capital Structures Fd. Ltd. v. Stillwater Mining Co.*, 240 A.3d 3 (Del. 2020).

---

*   Page 994 at bottom of page of the Condensed Edition.

E. THE STOCK MODES AND THE DE FACTO MERGER THEORY

Page 1356.* Add the following after current note 2:

3.   Note on "Divisive Merger" and Its Role in the "Texas Two-Step" in Bankruptcy. As we have seen, in a traditional merger two or more entities merge to become a single entity; the reverse of this is the relatively new development of the "divisive merger" whereby an entity divides itself into multiple entities. A further distinction is that the dividing entity's existence does not terminate, but continues as a surviving entity. The assets, liabilities and obligations of the dividing entity are allocated among the new entities formed pursuant to the merger and the surviving entity, if applicable. Texas is in the vanguard of states authorizing divisive mergers, doing so by defining mergers to include transactions undertaken to divide a company into distinct entities. *See* Texas Bus. Org. Code § 1.002(55)(A). Delaware authorizes divisive mergers only for LLCs. *See* Del. L.L.C. Act § 18–217. To effect a divisive merger, the dividing entity must adopt a plan of merger that sets forth the allocation of the dividing entity's assets and liabilities among the surviving entity (if applicable) and the entities formed pursuant to the division. Of special note in the Texas provision is that the divisive merger does not result in "any transfer or assignment having occurred." This provision has the potential of insulating the transaction from legal challenges founded on notions of it being a fraudulent conveyance, i.e., a transfer made without sufficient consideration while insolvent.

Firms facing significant product liability claims have found solace, at least momentarily, through resort to the Texas divisive merger provision. In doing so, they have focused attention on a strategy dubbed "the Texas Two-Step."

> Johnson & Johnson has a problem. For decades, it sold talc baby powder, a product that made Johnson & Johnson a household name and earned the business billions. But then, as those babies grew up, they started getting cancer. And then they began suing. Last June, twenty-two plaintiffs cemented a $2.12 billion judgment against Johnson & Johnson for cancer caused by its baby powder. Another thirty-four thousand cases (and counting) remain in progress, each with the potential for a similar verdict.
>
> To handle these mass-tort liabilities, Johnson & Johnson has followed the lead of many businesses and turned to the bankruptcy courts. But it has done so with a twist. Unlike the businesses that pioneered using bankruptcy for mass torts, Johnson & Johnson is not filing for bankruptcy. It is instead dividing itself using an obscure Texas law, moving its assets into one business and its talc liabilities into another, and having the liability-laden business file for bankruptcy. This maneuver, known as the "Texas Two-Step," threatens the tort recovery of tens of thousands of talc claimants.

---

*   Page 1011 in the Concise Edition.

Michael A. Francus, Texas Two-Stepping Out of Bankruptcy (Jan. 31, 2022). Available at https://ssrn.com/abstract=4021502.

It remains to be seen how courts will ultimately resolve whether such as that engineered by Johnson & Johnson can reverse centuries of creditor protections, e.g. fraudulent conveyance acts, against debtors aggressively seeking to unilaterally discharge themselves of their obligations. This uncertainty arises in light that a fundamental rule of contract law is that an obligor or debtor cannot get rid of an obligation or debt by assigning it to a third person. We therefore see the significance of provisions, such as that in Texas, where it appears the legislature seeks to overcome this well-received axiom by deeming there is no transfer. What other reasons might prompt a business to undertake a divisive merger?

G. FREEZEOUTS

Page 1384.[*] **Insert the following after the end of** *Kahn v. Lynch Communication Systems*:

Flood v. Synutra Int'l, Inc.

Supreme Court of Delaware, 2018.
195 A.3d 754.

■ STRINE, CHIEF JUSTICE, for the Majority.

Liang Zhang and entities related to him controlled 63.5% of Synutra International Inc.'s stock. In January 2016, Zhang proposed to take Synutra private by acquiring the rest of the stock he did not control. In an initial letter, Zhang proposed purchasing the remaining shares at $5.91, but he did not include a requirement that the sale be conditioned on the approval of a special committee and an affirmative vote of a majority of the minority stockholders. . . .

One week after Zhang issued his proposal, the Board met and formed a Special Committee. Before the meeting, the Board "agreed that it would not substantively evaluate" Zhang's proposal. . . .

Two weeks after the initial offer, and only one week after the Special Committee was formed, Zhang sent a second letter to the Special Committee stipulating that he would not proceed with the transaction unless it was approved by the Special Committee and approved by the holders of a majority of the voting stock not controlled by Zhang. No negotiations had commenced as of that time; the Special Committee had not met and the complaint is devoid of any facts suggesting that the Special Committee and Zhang had engaged in any economic negotiations. In fact, the plaintiff's complaint makes clear that:

- the Special Committee did not engage its own investment bank or counsel until after this point;

---

[*]   Page 1035 of Subsection F of the Condensed Edition.

- the Special Committee declined to engage in price negotiations until its banker could do due diligence and obtain projections; and

- the price negotiations did not begin until seven months after Zhang's second offer conditioning any merger on both Special Committee and majority-of-the-minority approval.

Thus, the plaintiff does not allege any negotiations or other meetings occurred before Zhang's second offer, which conditioned the take-private offer on *MFW*'s dual requirements. . . .

After receiving Zhang's second offer—proposing the same price as the first offer—on January 30, 2016, the Special Committee hired Houlihan Lokey and Cleary Gottlieb as its independent financial and legal advisors. Houlihan began discussions with management regarding the company's financial projections. On March 22, 2016, Houlihan met with the company's CFO to discuss what was needed for Houlihan to advise the Special Committee. . . .

The plaintiff grounds its argument in the language of our opinion in *MFW* that says both procedural protections must be in place "*ab initio*" (Latin for "from the beginning"), and in language from the Court of Chancery's decision in *MFW* that uses the phrase "[f]rom inception." . . .

[T]he plaintiff argues that, because Zhang's initial offer letter did not contain the Special Committee approval and majority-of-the-minority vote conditions, the business judgment rule does not apply. In the plaintiff's view, if a controller's first approach does not contain the required conditions, then it is stuck with entire fairness review, even if the controller still commits itself to *MFW*'s requirements early on before any economic negotiations. . . .

[The plaintiff's interpretation of MFW] is at odds with the origins of why that decision requires that the controller condition its offer early in the process—i.e., before any substantive economic negotiations begin—on the two key procedural protections. . . .

[T]he purpose of the words "*ab initio*," and other formulations like it in the *MFW* decisions, require the controller to self-disable before the start of substantive economic negotiations, and to have both the controller and Special Committee bargain under the pressures exerted on both of them by these protections. Thus, so long as the controller conditions its offer on the key protections at the germination stage of the Special Committee process, when it is selecting its advisors, establishing its method of proceeding, beginning its due diligence, and has not commenced substantive economic negotiations with the controller, the purpose of the pre-condition requirement of *MFW* is satisfied. In that situation, the Special Committee and the controller know, at all times during economic bargaining, that a transaction cannot proceed if the Special Committee says no, and the Special Committee knows that if they agree to a price, their judgment will be subject to stockholder scrutiny and approval.

Thus, so long as the controller conditions its offer on the key protections at the germination stage of the Special Committee process, when it is selecting its advisors, establishing its method of proceeding, beginning its due diligence, and has not commenced substantive economic negotiations with the controller, the purpose of the pre-condition requirement of *MFW* is satisfied. In that situation, the Special Committee and the controller know, at all times during economic bargaining, that a transaction cannot proceed if the Special Committee says no, and the Special Committee knows that if they agree to a price, their judgment will be subject to stockholder scrutiny and approval. . . .

The Court of Chancery found that Zhang "sent the Follow-up Letter just over two weeks after [he] first proposed the Merger, before the Special Committee ever convened and before any negotiations ever took place. The prompt sending of the Follow-up Letter prevented [Zhang] from using the [*MFW*] conditions as bargaining chips." And the plaintiff pled no facts suggesting that the Special Committee or any member of the committee communicated with Zhang about the substance of the transaction before he sent the second letter. Indeed, Zhang disabled before the Special Committee had hired its advisors. And the Special Committee spent months working with its advisors before asking Zhang for additional consideration. All of the Special Committee's work was done after Zhang had agreed to condition his buyout on *MFW*'s dual requirement. Zhang thus conditioned the buyout at the beginning of the process and is therefore entitled review under the business judgment rule standard. . . .

■ VALIHURA, JUSTICE, dissenting: . . .

I differ with the views of my learned colleagues on the important question of what the test should be for invoking business judgment protection in controller buyout transactions. The Majority's adoption of the "when the negotiations begin" test invites factual inquiries that defeat the purpose of what should be more of a bright line and narrower pathway for pleading-stage dismissals in this context. Instead, I believe this Court did conclude in *M&F Worldwide*, and should reaffirm now, that in controller squeeze-out transactions where the controller is on both sides, the *ab initio* requirement is satisfied when the Dual Protections are contained in the controller's initial formal written proposal. This bright-line makes sense because the controller dictates when to commence the transactional process so that the outset is clear. . . .

* * *

NOTE ON SCOPE OF *KAHN V. M.W. WORLDWIDE*

Can a controller avoid the scrutiny of Delaware's "entire fairness review" standard without adhering to all the requirements of *Kahn*? *In re Tesla*

Motors, Inc. Shareholder Litig., 2020 Del. Ch. LEXIS 51 (Del. Ch. Feb. 4, 2020), holds entire fairness review applies even though the transaction with its controller was approved by an informed vote of the disinterested shareholders and there was no evidence the vote was coerced. Vice-Chancellor Slights reasoned:

> One of the fundamental purposes of the entire fairness standard of review is to provide a framework for this Court to review transactions involving conflicted controllers. A conflicted controller has strong incentives to engage in transactions that benefit him to the detriment of the corporation and its other stockholders. And, as an "800-pound gorilla" in the board room and at the ballot box, the controller has retributive capacities that lead our courts to question whether independent directors or voting shareholders can freely exercise their judgment in approving transactions sponsored by the controller. In these circumstances, shareholders are entitled to an independent review where the controller is made to explain why the transaction's process and price were fair.

> If the facts proven at trial demonstrate that Musk was Tesla's controller at the time of the Merger, Defendants will still avoid liability if the transaction was fair. Entire fairness review of the Merger is not a prejudgment that fiduciary misconduct occurred. It is simply a recognition that because conflicted controller transactions have such strong potential for self-dealing, absent replication of an arm's-length transaction process, an independent judge should thoroughly examine the transaction's substantive fairness.

Among the disputed issues was whether Elon Musk, the owner of 22.1 percent of Tesla's voting stock was in control. Delaware's focus on this issue is "the ability to control rather than the actual exercise of control." Id. at 5, whereby courts consider a variety of factors such as whether the CEO (Musk) was a "hands on" manager and an "inspirational force" within the firm.

2.   Hostile Takeovers and Defending Control

A.   The Williams Act

Page 1404.* Insert the following to the end of note 1:

In early 2022, the SEC, proposed a series of important changes to the early warning provisions set forth in Section 13(d) of the Exchange Act. The most significant proposed changes are:

> Shorten the period to five days (from ten days) in which a person has to file Schedule 13D or Schedule 13G (in the case of passive investors) after becoming a beneficial owner of more than 5 percent of the equity securities of a reporting company.

---

*   Page 1055 in the Concise Edition.

Expanding the meaning of "beneficial owner" to include ownership of certain cash-settled derivatives that are acquired with control in mind.

Setting forth a means whereby two or more persons can communicate and consult with one another and engage with a target without concern they must make a filing under Section 13(d).

SEC, Modernization of Beneficial Ownership Reporting, Securities Act Rel. No. 11030 (Feb. 10, 2022).

C. POISON PILLS

Page 1427.* Insert the following immediately before *Air Products and Chemicals, Inc. v. Airgas, Inc.*

The Williams Companies Stockholder Litigation
Court of Chancery of Delaware, 2021.
2021 LEXIS 34 (Del. Ch., Feb. 26, 2021), *aff'd, The Williams Companies, Inc. v. Wolosky,* 264 A.3d 641 (Del. 2021) (en banc).

■ McCORMICK, V.C.

This litigation concerns the validity of a stockholder rights plan [the "Plan"], or so-called "poison pill," a device that came to popularity in the 1980s as a response to front-end loaded, two-tiered tender offers. Coercive tender offers of the 1980s were "to takeovers what the forward pass was to Notre Dame football in the days of Knute Rockne," and a powerful offense required a powerful defense. Of all the defenses developed to fend off hostile takeovers, the poison pill was among the most muscular. These bulwarks gained judicial imprimatur in 1985 when the Delaware Supreme Court upheld a poison pill as an antitakeover device in *Moran v. Household International, Inc. Moran* also established intermediate scrutiny under *Unocal* as the legal framework for reviewing stockholder challenges to poison pills.

Poison pills metamorphosed post-*Moran*. The flip-over feature of the *Moran* pill was augmented by a flip-in feature. After the adoption of state anti-takeover statutes, trigger thresholds crept down from the 20% threshold of *Moran* to 15% and then to 10% in some instances. The pill's initial success engendered mission creep. Originally conceived as anti-takeover armaments, poison pills were redirected to address other corporate purposes such as protecting net operating loss [NOL] assets. Recently, pills have been deployed to defend against stockholder activism.

The plaintiffs in this litigation challenge an anti-activist pill adopted by the board of directors of The Williams Companies, Inc. ("Williams" or the "Company") at the outset of the COVID-19 pandemic and amid a global oil price war. The Williams pill is unprecedented in that it contains

---

*   Page 1078 in the Concise Edition.

a more extreme combination of features than any pill previously evaluated by this court—a 5% trigger threshold, an expansive definition of "acting in concert," and a narrow definition of "passive investor."

. . . The defendants identify three supposed threats: first, the desire to prevent stockholder activism during a time of market uncertainty and a low stock price, although the Williams board was not aware of any specific activist plays afoot; second, the apprehension that hypothetical activists might pursue "short-term" agendas or distract management from guiding Williams through uncertain times; and third, the concern that activists might stealthily and rapidly accumulate over 5% of Williams stock [in light of "gaps" in the federal disclosure regime (*i.e.,* Section 13(d) of the Exchange Act and the pre-merger notification provisions of the Hart-Scott-Rodino Act)].

Of these three threats, the first two run contrary the tenet of Delaware law that directors cannot justify their actions by arguing that, without board intervention, the stockholders would vote erroneously out of ignorance or mistaken belief. This decision assumes for the sake of analysis that the third threat presents a legitimate corporate objective but concludes that the Company's response was not proportional and enjoins the Williams pill. . . .

[The Williams board adopted the Plan following stock price volatility caused by COVID-19 and a global oil price war.]

H. The Plan's Features

The Plan will expire at the end of one year and has four key features: (i) a 5% trigger; (ii) a definition of "acquiring person" that captures beneficial ownership as well as ownership of certain derivative interests, such as warrants and options; (iii) an "acting in concert" provision that extends to parallel conduct and includes a "daisy chain" concept (the "AIC Provision"); and (iv) a limited "passive investor" exemption. . . .

1. The 5% Trigger

The Plan established a trigger threshold of "5% or more." The Plan is triggered, and the rights distributed, on "the close of business on the tenth Business Day after" a "Person" (defined as an individual, firm, or entity) acquires "beneficial ownership" of 5% or more of Williams stock or commences "a tender or exchange offer" that would result in their ownership reaching that threshold. Given Williams' market capitalization in March 2020, triggering the 5% threshold at the time the Plan was adopted would have required an economic investment (sometimes referred to as a "toehold") of approximately $650 million.

2. Beneficial Ownership Definition

The Plan's definition of "beneficial ownership" starts with the definition found in Rule 13d–3 of the Exchange Act, then extends more broadly to include "[c]ertain synthetic interests in securities created by derivative positions," such as warrants and options.

3. The AIC Provision

The AIC Provision deems a Person to be "Acting in Concert" with another Person if:

> such Person knowingly acts (whether or not pursuant to an express agreement, arrangement or understanding) at any time after the first public announcement of the adoption of this Right Agreement, in concert or in parallel with such other Person, or towards a common goal with such other Person, relating to changing or influencing the control of the Company or in connection with or as a participant in any transaction having that purpose or effect, where (i) each Person is conscious of the other Person's conduct and this awareness is an element in their respective decision-making processes and (ii) at least one additional factor supports a determination by the Board that such Persons intended to act in concert or in parallel, which additional factors may include exchanging information, attending meetings, conducting discussions, or making or soliciting invitations to act in concert or in parallel.

Breaking it down, the AIC Provision deems a Person to be "Acting in Concert" with another where the Person: (1) "knowingly acts ... in concert or in parallel ... or towards a common goal" with another; (2) if the goal "relat[es] to changing or influencing the control of the Company or [is] in connection with or as a participant in any transaction having that purpose or effect;" (3) where each Person is "conscious of the other Person's conduct" and "this awareness is an element in their respective decision-making processes;" and (4) there is the presence of at least one additional factor to be determined by the Board, "which additional factors may include exchanging information, attending meetings, conducting discussions, or making or soliciting invitations to act in concert or in parallel." The fourth factor of this definition gives the Board "a great amount of latitude" for making the "Acting in Concert" determination.

The "parallel-conduct" dimension of the "acting in concert" provision (sometimes referred to as a "wolfpack" provision) is a feature of modern pills, ... [P]oison pills have always included an acting-in-concert concept. Early poison pills required express agreements, using language that tracked the definitions of a "group," "affiliate," and "associate" under Section 13(d) and Rule 12b–2 of the Exchange Act. Express agreement provisions do not capture so-called wolfpack activism achieved through " 'conscious parallelism' that deliberately stop[s] short of an explicit agreement."

The AIC Provision includes a "daisy chain" concept, providing that "[a] Person who is Acting in Concert with another Person shall be deemed to be Acting in Concert with any third party who is also Acting in Concert with such other Person." Put differently, stockholders act in concert with one another by separately and independently "Acting in Concert" with the same third party. . . .

The AIC Provision does not apply to a public proxy solicitation or tender offer. Persons are not deemed to be "Acting in Concert" solely as a result of soliciting proxies in connection with a "public proxy or consent solicitation made to more than 10 holders of shares of a class of stock" or when soliciting tenders pursuant to a "public tender or exchange offer." While this provision allows stockholders to initiate a proxy contest and solicit proxies without triggering the Plan, it does not exempt routine communications among stockholder before the launch of a proxy contest or tender offer.

The AIC Provision is also asymmetrical. It excludes "actions by an officer or director of the Company acting in such capacities," such that incumbents can act in concert without suffering the consequences of the Plan. . . .

II. LEGAL ANALYSIS

Plaintiffs claim that the Director Defendants breached their fiduciary duties when adopting and maintaining the Plan. . . .

"Modern corporate law recognizes that stockholders have three fundamental, substantive rights: to vote, to sell, and to sue."[228] From these fundamental rights flow subsidiary rights, including the right to communicate with other stockholders, nominate directors, and communicate with (and even oppose) management and the Board. As this court has observed, "[o]ne of the basic rights of a stockholder is to be able to communicate with his fellow stockholders on matters germane to such stock, and, if necessary, to organize other stockholders for corporate action."[231]

All rights plans interfere to some degree with the right to sell and the right to vote, but *Moran* held that the level of interference is nominal in the traditional anti-takeover pill that has both a relatively high trigger and an exception for soliciting revocable proxies. A traditional pill did not attempt to restrict stockholder communications. As discussed below, the Plan goes beyond a traditional pill by combining a parsimonious trigger of 5% with the AIC Provision . . . . Through this combination of provisions, the Plan limits the act of communicating itself, whether with other stockholders or management. It also restricts the stockholder's ability to nominate directors. It thus infringes on the stockholders' ability to communicate freely in connection with the stockholder franchise, much of which occurs outside the context of proxy contests. This articulation of the harm flows to stockholders and not the Company. . . . [Accordingly, the Court held that the plaintiffs' claim was direct, not derivative.] . . . .

---

[228] *Strougo v. Hollander*, 111 A.3d 590, 595 n.21 (Del. Ch. 2015).

[231] *B.F. Goodrich Co. v. Nw. Indus., Inc.*, 1969 WL 2932, at *2 (Del. Ch. Mar. 26, 1969).

C. The *Unocal* Analysis

... *Unocal* calls for a two-part inquiry. "The first part of *Unocal* review requires a board to show that it had reasonable grounds for concluding that a threat to the corporate enterprise existed." Framed more broadly, directors must demonstrate that they acted in good faith to achieve a "legitimate corporate objective." ...

To meet their burden under the first part of *Unocal*, however, Defendants must do more than show good faith and reasonable investigation. "[T]he first part of *Unocal* review requires more than that; it requires the board to show that its good faith and reasonable investigation *ultimately gave the board 'grounds for concluding that a threat to the corporate enterprise existed.'*" In other words, after conducting a reasonable investigation and acting in good faith, the board must show that it sought to serve a legitimate corporate objective by responding to a legitimate threat. If the threat is not legitimate, then a reasonable investigation into the illegitimate threat, or a good faith belief that the threat warranted a response, will not be enough to save the board.

The second part of *Unocal* requires a board to show that the defensive measures were "reasonable in relation to the threat posed." This element of the *Unocal* test recognizes that a board's powers to act "are not absolute" and that a board "does not have unbridled discretion to defeat any perceived threat by any Draconian means available." When applying the reasonableness standard, the court does not substitute its judgment for that of the board. The court instead determines whether the measure falls within "the range of reasonableness." ...

a. The Actual Threats That the Board Identified

[The court noted the difficulty of identifying "a unified purpose" behind a decision by the board, particularly in the context of litigation.] The materials ... all state that the Plan was intended in part to serve as a takeover deterrent. But the Plan was not designed for that purpose, and some of the directors did not have that in mind when adopting the Plan. The Plan was not adopted with the objective of deterring takeover attempts.

In fact, the Plan was not adopted to protect against any *specific* threat at all. The Board was not concerned about any specific activist threat. Nor was the Board acting to preserve any specific asset like an NOL. Instead, the Board was acting pre-emptively to interdict hypothetical future threats. ...

[Independent director] Cogut's testimony [concerning the reasons for adopting the Plan] was the most unadorned and refreshingly candid. He testified that he proposed the Plan to insulate the Board and management from all forms of stockholder activism during the uncertainty of the pandemic. In Cogut's words: ...

- The Plan's objective was agnostic regarding different kinds of activism. When asked whether Cogut was "drawing distinctions between different kinds of activism" the Plan was trying to halt, he responded: *"Any activism that would influence control over the company* at an aggregate level above 5 percent, yeah."

- The Plan's value was its ability "to prevent against an activist buying a toehold of 5 percent or more or acting in concert with other activists *so that our management could be freed up . . . to run a company during COVID."*

- The Plan's power was immense: "[T]he shareholder rights plan is the *nuclear weapon of corporate governance,"* and "nuclear weapons are deterrents" that would force activists to deal with the Board instead of talking to each other.

- The Plan's objective was to impose a *"one-year moratorium"* on activism. . . .

b. The Legitimacy of the Actual Threats

The first prong of *Unocal* requires evaluating whether the Board has demonstrated that it conducted a good faith reasonable investigation and had "grounds for concluding that a threat to the corporate enterprise existed." Defendants have demonstrated that the Board conducted a good faith, reasonable investigation when adopting the Plan. The Director Defendants are nearly all independent, outside directors. They considered the Plan over the course of two meetings. Although aspects of the record create the impression that the second Board meeting was window dressing, it is clear that there was genuine deliberation concerning the Plan. Defendants were advised by outside legal and financial advisors who were available to answer questions. Certainly, aspects of the process were less than perfect. Still, nothing about the process jumps out as unreasonable.

The real problem is not the process that Defendants followed, but the threats they identified. The first threat was quite general—the desire to prevent stockholder activism during a time of market uncertainty and a low stock price. The second threat was only slightly more specific—the concern that activists might pursue "short-term" agendas or distract management. The third threat was just a hair more particularized—the concern that activists might rapidly accumulate over 5% of the stock and the possibility that the Plan could serve as an early detection device to plug the gaps in the federal disclosure regime. Each of the three threats were purely hypothetical; the Board was not aware of any specific activist plays afoot. The question presented is whether these hypothetical threats present legitimate corporate objectives under Delaware law.

i. Stockholder Activism

"Stockholder activism" is a broad concept that refers to a range of stockholder activities intended to change or influence a corporation's direction. Activists may pressure a corporation to make management changes, implement operational improvements, or pursue a sale transaction. They may seek to catalyze or halt a merger or acquisition. More recently, "ESG activism" has come to the fore, and stockholders have begun pressuring corporations to adopt or modify policies to accomplish environmental, social, and governance goals. Many forms of stockholder activism can be beneficial to a corporation, as Defendants themselves recognize.

Under Delaware law, the board of directors manages the business and affairs of the corporation. Thus, stockholder activism is directed to the board. And activists' ability to replace directors through the stockholder franchise is the reason why boards listen to activists. Most activists hold far less than a hard majority of a corporation's stock, making the main lever at an activist's disposal a proxy fight. In this way, stockholder activism is intertwined with the stockholder franchise.

Under Delaware law, directors cannot justify their actions by arguing that "without their intervention, the stockholders would vote erroneously out of ignorance or mistaken belief" in an uncoerced, fully informed election. "The notion that directors know better than the stockholders about who should be on the board is no justification at all."

Viewing all stockholder activism as a threat is an extreme manifestation of the proscribed we-know-better justification for interfering with the franchise. That is, categorically concluding that all stockholder efforts to change or influence corporate direction constitute a threat to the corporation runs directly contrary to the ideological underpinnings of Delaware law. The broad category of conduct referred to as stockholder activism, therefore, cannot constitute a cognizable threat under the first prong of *Unocal*.

To be sure, Delaware law does not categorically foreclose the possibility that certain conduct by activist stockholders might give rise to a cognizable threat. . . . [However, the Court concluded that the Board's generalized concern about stockholder activism failed to constitute a cognizable threat under *Unocal*.]

ii. Short-Termism and Distraction

The Board's second concern was that activists might pursue short-term agendas or disrupt or distract management. The "short-termism" justification refers to the concern that "a particular activist seeks short-term profit without regard to the impact on the company's long-term prospects." The "disruption" justification typically refers to the concern that the actions of the activists might cause operational disruption . . . . Here, the Director Defendants instead frame this concern as a desire to insulate the management team from distraction.

No case has evaluated under *Unocal* whether these types of particularized activist concerns constitute cognizable threats. . . .

Reasonable minds can dispute whether short-termism or distraction could be deemed cognizable threats under Delaware law. These sorts of justifications, particularly short-termism, are conspicuous in the policy debate, but they become nebulous when viewed through a doctrinal lens. The central criticism of short-termism is that "shareholders who favor short-termism . . . are hurting themselves as much as they are hurting their fellow shareholders." This is a valid policy argument, but as one group of scholars have commented, the " 'short-termism' argument just particularizes the concern that shareholders will cast votes in a mistaken assessment of their own best interests." That is, short-termism and distraction concerns boil down to the sort of we-know-better justification that Delaware law eschews in the voting context.

Although there is room to disagree as to whether short-termism or distraction could be deemed cognizable threats under Delaware law, this decision does not resolve that issue. Even if justifications of short-termism or disruption could rise to the level of a cognizable threat, hypothetical versions of these justifications cannot. The concerns in this case are raised in the abstract—there is no "specific, immediate" activist play seeking short-term profit or threatening disruption. When used in the hypothetical sense untethered to any concrete event, the phrases "short-termism" and "disruption" amount to mere euphemisms for stereotypes of stockholder activism generally and thus are not cognizable threats. . . .

2. The Proportionality of the Response

Because Plaintiffs do not claim that the Plan is coercive or preclusive, the second prong of the *Unocal* inquiry requires the court to evaluate whether Defendants proved that adopting the Plan fell within a range of reasonable responses to the lightning-strike threat posed.

The thirty-thousand-foot view looks bad for Defendants. As Morgan Stanley advised the Board at the March 19 Meeting, the 5% trigger alone distinguished the Plan; only 2% of all plans identified by Morgan Stanley had a trigger lower than 10%. . . . Of the twenty-one pills adopted between March 13 and April 6, 2020, only the Plan had a 5% triggering threshold. Of the twenty-one companies that adopted pills during that time, thirteen faced ongoing activist campaigns when adopting their pill.

The Plan's other key features are also extreme. . . .

The Plan's features . . . raise concerns . . . . As Plaintiffs' proxy solicitor testified at trial, the Plan's combination of features are likely to chill a wide range of anodyne stockholder communications. Although the 5% trigger is a marked departure from market norms, it is not the most problematic aspect of the Plan, because a 5% ownership limit still permits an activist to buy a larger dollar value toehold in Williams than the vast majority of other poison pills with higher triggers. The primary offender is the AIC Provision, whose broad language sweeps up potentially benign stockholder communications "relating to changing *or influencing* the control of the Company." The definition gives the Board discretion to determine whether "plus" factors as innocuous as "exchanging information, attending meetings, [or] conducting discussions" can trigger the Plan. This language encompasses routine activities such as attending investor conferences and advocating for the same corporate action. It gloms on to this broad scope the daisy-chain concept that operates to aggregate stockholders even if members of the group have no idea that the other stockholders exist. . . .

In the end, Defendants "bear the burden to show their actions were reasonable." They have failed to show that this extreme, unprecedented collection of features bears a reasonable relationship to their stated corporate objective. Because Defendants failed to prove that the Plan falls within the range of reasonable responses, the Plan is invalid. . . .

D. THE "REVLON MOMENT"

Page 1473.* Insert the following after *Sciabacucchi v. Liberty Broadband Corp.*:

NOTE ON THE RISE OF FINANCIAL INSTITUTIONS AND THE DECLINE IN JUDICIAL REVIEW

As seen in Chapter 5, a high percentage of the equity of large publicly traded companies is owned by financial institutions, with 20 percent of all publicly traded equity is held by index funds. Indeed, Big Three fund managers—Vanguard, Blackrock and State Street—have garnered 70 percent of the substantial flow of investor money committed to a passive investment strategy. The concentration of such voting power in the hands of large sophisticated financial institutions may well explain many developments in Delaware, such as *Corwin* and *M.F. Worldwide* whereby governance anchored in the shareholder vote displaces ex post judicial review as the bulwark for protecting investors.

> The transformation of American equity markets from retail to institutional ownership has relocated control over corporations from courts to markets and has led to the death of corporate law. As a result . . . Delaware courts today play a fundamentally different—and much less influential—role in corporate disputes. . . . ". . .[T]he more competent shareholders become, the less important corporate law will be. This is why the dramatic rise of institutional ownership in the United States coincided with the eclipse of corporate law." Zohar Goshen & Sharon Hannes, The Death of Corporate Law, 94 N.Y.U. L. Rev. 263, 265 & 269 (2019)

The disciplining hand of sophisticated shareholder in such a world has a good deal of intuitive appeal. However, not all commentators are so sanguine regarding the role of today's institutions to so self protect. Consider the pattern described in the next two excerpts.

---

*   Page 1117 in the Condensed Edition.

We believe that a shareholder vote, such as that which is celebrated in *Corwin*, is misunderstood and that according it with insulating misconduct surrounding the approved transaction not only misinterprets the import of the vote but also distorts the corporate governance developments reviewed above. As such, the emphasis on a shareholder vote unduly insulates from judicial review director and officer failures to act as trustworthy stewards in the sale of their company.

One factor that looms large in our thinking is the overwhelming frequency with which shareholders are relied upon to approve complex—and often conflicted—transactions. If shareholder approval of the deal is the first—and, per *Corwin*, the only—line of defense to managerial misconduct in connection with M&A transactions, we would expect that activist investors would be regularly turning down bad deals. In fact, the record of shareholder voting on such matters is at best ponderous. Empirically, shareholders rarely vote down mergers. We can illustrate this point using data from Professor Morgan Ricks's database on mergers and acquisitions. His data cover all mergers and acquisitions involving U.S. public company targets undertaken after January 1, 1996, and concluded by March 31, 2017. The minimum-size deals included in the database is $1 billion, and there are a total of 1,620 deals included in it. In all, only five deals were rejected by shareholders in a formal vote. In other words, a total of 0.3 percent of all mergers have a failed shareholder vote. An additional seventeen deals were withdrawn before completion, some of which may have been withdrawn because of an anticipated negative shareholder vote. If all twenty-two transactions are counted as shareholder-rejected deals—which is certainly an overestimate—then only 1.3 percent of large mergers fail from lack of shareholder approval.

Other data sets yield the same result. For example, from a universe of fifty going-private transactions instigated by controlling shareholders between 2010 and 2017, Professor Ed Rock isolated seventeen in which the transaction was conditioned on approval by a majority of the minority holders. In none of those transactions did the minority shareholders reject the transaction.[1] Moreover, in his analysis of some of the going-private transactions that involved the agitation against the transaction by an activist hedge fund, Professor Rock noted that all of them ultimately resulted in the activist investors accepting the deal. He explained this as reflecting that activists had no better means to exit from the target company than the one provided by the controlling stockholder.[2]

---

[1]   Edward B. Rock, *Majority of the Minority Approval in a World of Active Shareholders*, *in* THE LAW AND FINANCE OF RELATED PARTY TRANSACTIONS 105, 115–17 (Luca Enriques & Tobias H. Tröger eds., 2019).

[2]   *Id.* at 129–31.

Finally, there is strong empirical evidence that indicates "management wins all of the close" votes in situations where the board of directors is submitting management proposals for shareholder approval.[3] Professor Listokin's study "examines votes on management-sponsored resolutions and finds widespread irregularities in the distribution of votes received by management."[4] He further notes: "Management is overwhelmingly more likely to win votes by a small margin than lose by a small margin. The results indicate that, at some point in the voting process, management obtains highly accurate information about the likely voting outcome and, based on that information, acts to influence the vote."[5] . . .

The above record of the low percentage of shareholder "NO" votes is equally supportive of two distinct but opposing propositions: (1) the shareholder vote means nothing as they blindly support the deal or, if not blind, will prefer the sparrow in the hand over the pheasant in the bush; or (2) all deals are great deals because the prospect of a vote by the shareholders chastens managers and self-dealing directors to think twice before they submit a suboptimal deal for shareholder approval. . . .

James D. Cox, Tomas J. Mondino & Randall S. Thomas, Understanding the (Ir)Relevance of Shareholder Votes on M&A Deals, 69 Duke L. J. 503, 511–513 (2019).

Consider further the following regarding the voting record of the Big Three:

Consider the proxy voting guidelines that the Big Three follow in determining whether to support incumbent directors standing for reelection or to withhold their support. Each of the Big Three's guidelines lists situations and conditions that would lead to a withhold vote. Our review of these guidelines indicates that, for each of the Big Three, the important decision whether to support a director or withhold support is based exclusively on the existence or absence of certain divergences from good governance principles.

For example, Vanguard's proxy voting guidelines call for withholding votes from one or more directors if the board or a specific director deviates from certain governance principles in one or more specified ways, such as: (i) the board failing to have a majority of independent directors; (ii) the board failing to have audit, compensation, nominating, or governance committees that are fully independent; (iii) a specific director serving on five or more public company boards; or (iv) a specific director failing to attend more than 75% of board or committee meetings. BlackRock and

---

[3]   Yair Listokin, *Management Always Wins the Close Ones*, 10 AM. L. & ECON. REV. 159, 172–75 (2008).

[4]   *Id.* at 159.

[5]   *Id.*

SSGA's approaches differ in some details but are similarly based on comparison with good governance principles.

Furthermore, the Big Three Stewardship Reports indicate that the Big Three's private, behind-the-scenes engagements—when they do occur—also focus on companies that diverge significantly from desirable governance principles. For example, SSGA indicates that its engagement seeks to provide "principles-based guidance." BlackRock indicates that its engagement might occur when a company lags behind its peers on environmental, social, or governance matters; when it is in a sector with a thematic governance issue material to value; or for other reasons that do not include financial underperformance. Vanguard in turn states that its stewardship focuses on board composition, governance structures, executive compensation, and board processes for oversight of risk and strategy.

In assessing this focus on divergences from governance principles, we do not question the relevance and importance of such divergences for voting or engagement decisions. It is clearly valuable to take information regarding such divergences into account. In our view, however, value maximizing decisions on these matters would also require consideration of other types of information. . . . [B]elow, value-maximizing voting and engagement decisions would also incorporate detailed information about the business performance of the portfolio company and the qualifications, expertise, and experience of its directors.

Importantly, the proxy voting guidelines of the Big Three call for consideration of detailed company-specific information regarding business performance and the characteristics of particular directors in the case of a proxy contest over director elections between incumbents and a challenger's competing slate. To illustrate, for such contested director elections, Vanguard's proxy voting guidelines call for "case-by-case" decisions based on considerations including "[h]ow . . . the company [has] performed relative to its peers," and the extent to which the incumbent directors are "well-suited to address the company's needs" compared with the directors proposed by the challenger. The proxy voting guidelines of BlackRock and SSGA similarly call for using such information for voting in contested elections. But as we make clear above, the proxy voting guidelines of each of the Big Three do not call for using such considerations and information where the Big Three decide whether to support directors not facing a proxy challenger, which constitute the vast majority of their voting decisions.

Lucian Bebchuk & Scott Hirst, Index Funds and the Future of Corporate Governance: Theory, Evidence, and Policy, 119 Colum. L. Rev. 2029, 2090–2091 (2019).

Professors Bebchuk and Hirst further reason that passive investment managers have weak incentives to monitor the performance of their portfolio companies. The authors reason that stewardship investment whereby the funds monitor the financial performance of portfolio companies will not affect the level of assets under their management and thus not lead to the advisors garnering increased income. This conclusion is based in part on significant free rider problems that arise when Investor A incurs non-trivial costs to boost the performance and hence value of Company X; other indexed funds will accordingly benefit from that increase but without incurring the costs to improve Company X's performance. Moreover, they show that increased fees from value-adding stewardship would be too minimal to provide an incentive to managers to exercise meaningful and devoted oversight of the stewardship of individual portfolio companies because the gain they would thereby capture is but a small fraction of the gain their activities would provide. They then marshal data that supports this hypothesis. *Id.* 2050–2055. The focus of advisors who manage passive funds is not picking winners and losers but balancing the portfolio to reflect its weight in the identified index that lures fund investors. Thus, among those pursuing passive investments strategies there is cause to believe fund managers are indifferent to firm performance.